Logged On
and Tuned Out

nontechie's guide to parenting

tech-savvy generation

Vicki Courtney

PUBLISHING GROUP

nashville. tennessee

ISBN: 978-0-8054-4665-4

Published by B&H Publishing Group
Nashville, Tennessee

Dewey Decimal Classification: 649.1
Subject Heading: PARENTING
\ COMPUTERS AND CHILDREN \
INTERNET AND CHILDREN VISUAL
COMMUNICATION \ ONLINE SOCIAL
NETWORKS

Unless otherwise noted all Scripture is taken from the HCSB, Holman Christian Standard Bible®, copyright 1999, 2000, 2002, 2003 Holman Bible Publishers. Also used is NIV, New International Version, copyright © 1973, 1978, 1984 by International Bible Society and NLT, Holy Bible, New Living Translation, copyright © 1996. Used by permission of Tyndale House Publishers, Inc.

1 2 3 4 5 6 7 8   10 09 08 07

Contents

117563

Acknowledgments

I always feel slightly ill at ease when I see one of my books sitting on the bookstore shelf with my name emblazoned on the front cover. Perhaps it is because I know better than to think one person is responsible for a beautiful finished product that humbly began as a series of Word documents totaling thirty-five thousand words. That said, I am grateful that the acknowledgments allow me the opportunity to give credit where credit is due.

I love my publisher. Over the past several years, I have had the privilege of getting to know many of the B&H folks beyond their job titles and trust me when I say, these guys are the real deal. Their devotion to the craft is unmistakable, but I am most impressed with their honest sincerity to see a book become more than just words on a page. Much of what I write is a purging of sorts to encourage a much-needed change regarding the culture's negative influences on our children. The B&H crew gets it. I am forever grateful that they have partnered with me in sharing the mission as well as the message. As a newbie author, I honestly don't have a clue as to what actually goes on behind the scenes after a manuscript is e-mailed to the editor. I am more than aware that there are many players, most of whom I have never had the privilege of meeting. I think of the countless sales reps that pitch my books to bookstore buyers, whether it be the small mom-and-pop stores or the Super Wal-Marts. I think of the design team that works on the cover and labors over fonts and color palettes. I think of the folks who are bidding for end caps and product placement ads. To all of you, I say thank you, thank you.

Allow me to brag on a few of the B&H crew whom I've had the privilege of witnessing their work in action over the years. To my editors, Len Goss and Kim Overcash Stanford, thank you for always extending me grace with my deadlines when my schedule gets out of control. Even now, (throat clearing), you (Kim) are anxiously awaiting these acknowledgments and I am grateful for your never-ending patience.

I know there is a reason your co-workers have dubbed you, "she who must be obeyed," so I will stay up all night to get this done if need be! To Robin Patterson and Bonnie Batey, thank you for all you do to dream up the best marketing strategies ever. To the sales manager extraordinaire, David O'Brien; wow, your energy and enthusiasm amaze me. Thank you for being in my corner. To John Thompson and Craig Featherstone, thank you for your sincere desire as concerned parents to get this word out to other concerned parents. Craig, never switch to de-caf. Your enthusiasm is contagious, my friend. To Ken Stephens and David Shepherd, thank you for believing in what I do, and most of all, for your friendship. I will never forget how special you made me feel on the night we won the Christian Book Award and the impromptu dessert celebration that followed. You made me feel like I was part of the B&H family.

To my Literary Agent, Lee Hough, thank you for giving me your word that you never plan to retire. I wrote it down on the day you said it, and I will continue to remind you of that promise in the years to come. Keith and I are both very grateful for your attention to the details and ability to do a job that outgrew us long ago.

To the Virtuous Reality staff: Shelley, Shawna, Susan, Lindsey, and Michele—I honestly could not write books were it not for you. Because of your willingness to use your God-given abilities, I can rest assured that things are running smoothly when it comes to our events, virtuousreality.com, my blog page (virtuealert.com), etc. Thank you for wearing whatever hat is necessary to accomplish the task at hand. Lindsey, as my assistant, I cannot thank you enough for being the kind of assistant who practically reads my mind. You will never know what peace of mind it brings in my life knowing you're on top of my calendar, speaking requests, interviews, travel details, and the list goes on. You have spoiled me with those awesome travel packets you put together before each of my engagements!

To my husband, Keith, thank you for picking up the slack on the home front so I can write unencumbered. OK, so maybe you didn't have much to offer in the way of advice when it comes to technology, but your non-techie ways sure helped me better relate to the general audience! I confess that I find it adorably cute that you only use two fingers when typing away on your keyboard even though the kids and I poke fun at you on occasion. Bless your heart, I will laugh forever about the time you clicked the wrong button on Amazon and accidentally bought me a paddle boat for $1,100. Stories like that are living proof that this book is needed—without me, you would still be trying to figure out how to cancel that order! I am blessed beyond belief to be your bride. I cannot wait to grow old with you and sit on our porch swing at the lake house. You are truly my best friend.

Ah, and I could never forget my three wonderful children, Ryan, Paige, and Hayden. I know it is not easy having a mom who writes on teen culture and, especially, the subject of teens' logged-on lives. Thank you for allowing me to share real-life stories that involve your own experiences with technology. Thank you also for your never-ending patience when I camped out for months on MySpace and Facebook while researching for this book. My observations spawned many teachable moments and a few rant sessions over what teens were posting and you patiently endured them all. You are all troopers and it goes without saying that I am honored to be not only your mom, but your Facebook friend as well.

Finally, I could never acknowledge anything of merit without acknowledging my Lord and Savior, Jesus Christ. Without him, I am nothing and I have nothing of value to say. How I long for the world to know of his goodness.

Introduction

Parents, it's 10:00 p.m. Do you know where your children are? If you're from my generation, you might remember the public service announcement that was a common prelude to the evening news. As a mere child tucked safely away in my bed in the next room, I remember thinking, *How could parents not know where their child is?* Fast-forward to today, and the slogan takes on a whole new meaning. Our children live in an age when it's possible for them to be physically in the next room tapping away on a keyboard and yet mom and dad have no clue where they're going or to whom they're talking. Can you relate? Chances are, if you have a child in the home that is twelve years or older, you can. And if you're not there just yet, let this serve as a warning: it's coming down the pipe.

I'm betting that when you saw the title of the book, you assumed that the phrase "tuned out" was a reference to our logged-on children. Nope. That would be us—the hopelessly out-of-touch parents, who if the truth be told, just mastered checking our junk folders for missed e-mails that were mistaken for spam. Maybe you are a bit more tech savvy and have done some online shopping, uploaded your digital photos, and Googled your favorite restaurant to make reservations. You get extra credit if you have installed monitoring software (different from a safety filter) on your computers and set up Google alerts to your children's names. Stop right now and pat yourself on the back; you are among an elite few.

Some teens may deserve the tuned-out label, but for the most part studies show that their wired habits are not leaving them nearly as tuned out to life as we might think. They are commonly referred to as the "MySpace Generation," "Generation Y," or "IM Generation." Their greatest claim to fame is their ability to multitask between a multitude of technology forums. Just recently, I walked into my seventeen-year-old daughter's room while she was researching on her laptop for an English assignment. Within a matter of minutes, I watched her plug a term into a Google search to gather facts for the paper she was writing, toggle over to several IM screens and reply quickly to the messages received, toggle again back to the Google page to try another link, all the while, she has her ear buds in and is singing along to a song in her i-Tunes library. She is briefly interrupted by the buzz of a cell phone in her jeans pocket. She reads the text message and types a lightning fast response. Again, she turns her attention back to the computer screen. Amazing. I'm tired just watching her. And to think, this is the same child that can't seem to remember to wear her retainer at night.

Sound overwhelming? It might to you, but to teens it's just a normal part of their day. They have grown up adapting to technology as it changes, and at this rate it seems to change as often as the weather in Texas. And if what you just read above left you feeling light-headed and like you picked up a book on Mandarin Chinese, no worries—you will speak your child's wired language by the end of this book or at least enough of it to give you a passing grade in the course.

Before we get started, we need to recognize that the shift in technology is not just a trend or passing phase. The advancements we have seen in the last several years have not just changed the landscape of how our children communicate; they have set a new standard for how the majority of the public will communicate in the years to come. Like it or not, we can either learn now or learn later. While I know that our generation is somewhat resistant to change, we need to be open-minded enough to take an objective look at the changes in technology and the impact it has had on the way our children communicate.

Our nature as parents is to be suspicious of anything that challenges our way of life. Most of us have reached the point in life where we freeze-frame on a certain haircut, eat one brand of cereal in the morning for breakfast, and choose comfort over fashion when it comes to our wardrobes. We are old and we are dorks, as our children often remind us. And when it comes to technology, many of us sound like the same-old fuddy-duddy parents from the fifties who sat around and lamented about Elvis Presley's pelvic gyrations and ranted that it would surely summons the rapture. Let's not get so stuck in our ways that we fail to see any good in the way our teens communicate.

We can't afford to sit on the sidelines and grumble on this one; too much is at stake. So, what do you say? Will you join me in this crash course to better understand the technology-driven world in which our children live? Clearly you are a concerned and caring parent, or you wouldn't have picked up this book. I can't promise it will turn you into a technology genius, but it will equip you with enough knowledge to teach your kids to use technology in a responsible manner. Who knows, by the end you might be IMing, texting, blogging, and updating your very own MySpace page. And if you're really good, you can even watch a video clip of that Elvis guy on YouTube.

1

A Call for Parents to Log On and Tune In

I remember the exact moment when I realized I was completely and totally out of touch with my children's logged-on lives. My oldest child (now in college) was twelve years old at the time. Like most boys his age, he enjoyed playing an occasional game on the computer. Some games, like Sim City and Roller Coaster Tycoon, offered him an online outlet to use his creative abilities. What twelve-year-old wouldn't love designing his own city or theme park and building virtual homes and amusement park rides? I can't help but wonder if it was a factor in his declaring entrepreneurship as a major when he entered college.

At the time I found these games to be a welcome reprieve from the Mario theme song that was still ringing in my ears from his Nintendo phase of life. I thought I would never get that jingle out of my head. When it came to computer games, my knowledge ran dry after checking the approval rating on the front of the box. All that other gibberish about system requirements, blah, blah, blah, was left for my young son to figure out on his own. And figure it out he did. Like most other kids his age, he seemed to be hardwired from the womb to adapt to the constantly changing landscape of technology.

As for me, I was happy to stand by on the shoulder of the road and cheer him on as he lapped past me again and again on the information superhighway. Like most other adults my age, I prided myself on having mastered the task of sending and receiving e-mail, doing an occasional search for a product, and using Word to type my manuscripts. Anything beyond that would cause sweaty palms and increased heart palpitations. I was still part of the old school of thought that an accidental tap of the Escape key would result in the computer blowing up. I was content living my nontechie, ignorance-is-bliss existence—that is, until one afternoon when I received the wake-up call that would bring me out of my technological slumber.

My son had finished his homework and was playing a game on a computer we had set up on a desk area in the kitchen. I was busy doing other tasks when suddenly my son blurted out, "Yes! I won the checkers game!"

"Great!" I said. "Did you beat the computer?"

The answer that followed still makes a chill run up my spine. "No, I beat some guy in Canada." When he saw the look of sheer terror on my face, he added a quick, "Don't worry, Mom. He's a Christian." I tried not to hyperventilate as I made my way over to the computer. How in the world could my son be playing a game of checkers through this little metal box sitting right here in my kitchen with some guy thousands of miles away in Canada?

Let me also tell you that I was one of those mothers who was militant about giving my kids the "don't talk to strangers" talk. I had it covered from every angle. Don't help anyone find a lost pet; don't accept candy from strangers; don't give directions to anyone; don't go to the bathroom alone at movie theaters, the ball field, or any other public place, and on and on. I'm sure you can relate. On the top of every mother's list of fears regarding her children is the fear that her child will someday cross paths with a dreaded "stranger." I really thought I had done a good job in educating my children about strangers, that is, until this particular afternoon.

I began to ask my son rapid-fire questions: "How did you connect online to play checkers?" ("A friend showed me how"—a twelve-year-old at that!) "How do you know this person is from Canada?" ("Mom, the guy told me. You can type messages back and forth while you're playing.") "How do you know he's a Christian?" ("I asked him if he goes to church, and he said he did, and we started talking about that.") And finally, "What have I told you about talking to strangers?" ("Mom, this guy is not a stranger. He's just a guy who wants to play checkers!")

Instantly I was alarmed. After recovering from my shock, I had him show me just how he had managed to get online, find a checkers game, and begin playing checkers with complete strangers. His tutorial did not manage to calm me down, so I banned him from playing online games until I could get a better grasp on the situation.

I hardly had time to catch my breath when weeks later my son asked for permission to set up a screen name so he could IM back and forth with his friends. "A screen what?" I asked and then raced over to my bookshelf of parenting books and plucked the most current Dobson book off the shelf.

I flipped to the table of contents and began searching for the chapter detailing the appropriate age for instant messaging or safety tips for a game of online checkers. Nothing. It was as if overnight the landscape of parenting tweens and teens had shifted and parents were the last ones to get the memo. Then it dawned on me that I was on my own when it came to establishing appropriate rules and boundaries regarding the rapidly changing technology that was invading my children's lives. If not me, then who? In order to be an engaged and caring parent, it was time to face my fear and venture into the great unknown. And thus began my self-paced journey to better understand this new and ever-changing digital world in which our children live.

It was as if overnight the landscape of parenting tweens and teens had shifted and parents were the last ones to get the memo.

Fast-forward seven years and my son would be the first to tell you that his momma has come a long way since the online checkers incident. In fact, I have done hundreds of newspaper, radio, and TV interviews on the subject of Internet safety, as well as other issues pertaining to the digital world in which our tweens and teens live. I have a screen name, Google alerts set to my kids' names, and monitoring software installed on my home computers. I have added text messaging to my cell phone plan (though it takes me forever to send a message or reply). And yes, I even have a MySpace page, a Facebook page; and if the tide shifts to a newer and trendier social networking hangout for teens by the time you are reading this, I will likely have a page there too. By default of the fact that I write and speak on topics related to teen culture, I had to immerse myself into their digital world in an effort to "know my audience." And know them, I do. I know them more than I ever wanted to know them; and now I am happy to pass that information on to you, parent to parent, friend to friend.

Regardless of whether you have young kids who are tapping away on a Fisher-Price toy laptop, tweens who are begging for a real laptop, or teens who have taken over your laptop, you've picked up the right book. And we'll be covering far more than just the World Wide Web. We will address other forums of communication that bid for our preteens' and teens' attention. Before you let out a heavy sigh over the mere thought of trying to wrap your arms around this monumental task, let me assure you that the goal of this book is not to make your expert in technology. It is written from the perspective of an average mom who has learned plenty of things the hard way. I am not a parenting expert, nor do I claim to be an expert when it comes to technology. Everything I know, I learned by jumping in and tackling it head-on.

Let's face it—we all desire to be attentive and caring parents, but it becomes difficult when we can't possibly keep up with friend/buddy lists that number in the hundreds, unlimited text messages, instant messages, and the World Wide Web with more than 990 million users. Where are our children going online? To whom are they talking? Who is talking to them? Are they talking to strangers? Are they surfing porn sites? Do they have a MySpace or Facebook page? Are they texting while they are driving? Are they texting during school hours? Do they have trashy hip-hop songs loaded on their iPods? Are they addicted to online gaming sites? I wish we could take their annoying gadgets away! Let's go back to the pre-wired days where there were only three TV channels, cassette tapes that held about twelve songs, and a home phone tethered to the wall in the middle of the living room. At least then Mom and Dad had a good idea of who their kids' friends were and what they were up to because they were the mighty gatekeepers when the home phone rang. Nowadays, kids don't even know one another's home phone numbers because they have cell phones and can contact one another at all hours of the day or night. And what, may I ask you, is wrong with Pong, Atari, and PacMan? Our kids don't know what they're missing!

Let's face it—we are riding shotgun when it comes to technology. For years I have counted on my kids to change the ring tone on my cell phone or reboot the computer when the screen froze up. Is it really necessary to step in and get involved in their media-saturated worlds? You bet it is. The average teen spends more than seventy-two hours a week using electronic media (Internet, cell phones, television, music, and video games). Before you start doing the math and wondering how they fit in school and a few potty breaks, the study reflects that some of their devices overlap as they multitask their media intake.[1]

Let's face it—we are riding shotgun when it comes to technology.

Training Our Children to Use Technology Responsibly

I am witnessing a sense of desperateness among parents regarding technology and the impact it is having on their children. They want to be engaged and in the loop, but they don't have a clue where to begin. Again, it's not the intent of this book to turn parents into experts but rather to catch them up so they can train their children to use technology responsibly. With the influx of gadgets that enable our children to communicate instantly comes a tremendous obligation for someone to guide them to use technology in a responsible manner. After being in the trenches of teen culture and getting a behind-the-scenes glimpse of teens and their relationship with technology, it is clear to me that there are not enough chaperones at the party. Our kids are in desperate need of adult guidance, though few would willingly admit it. And they are more than aware that few parents can crack the code when it comes to infiltrating their wired worlds. It is literally a virtual free-for-all. Allowing them to learn as they go would be like handing a twelve-year-old car keys and telling him/her to run to the store for milk and bread. At night. In the bad part of town. No curfew in place. No experience necessary, no driver's ed. course, no permit period where they have to have a parent in the car. Just set them loose and wish them the best. Yet, essentially, that is what many parents have done when it comes to their preteens and teens and the technology they love. Just as there are rules for driving safely, the same is true for technology. Unless they are instructed properly, there is a high likelihood that they will be a hazard to themselves and others when they enter the ramp on the information superhighway.

Unless they are instructed properly, there is a high likelihood that they will be a hazard to themselves and others when they enter the ramp on the information superhighway.

The Need to Protect Them from Others

Let's stick with our driving analogy on this one. It doesn't matter how safe we are on the roads if we don't have a clue how to drive defensively. Every time we get behind the wheel, we subject ourselves to others on the road who should not be allowed on the road. The same is true when our kids log on to the computer and connect themselves to a world of dangers. We are so attentive in the early years to giving them the "don't talk to strangers" pep talk, but then we allow them to hang out with more than 990 million people who have access to the Internet!

Consider these recent findings from a study involving the online habits of teens, ages thirteen to seventeen:[2]

- 14 percent have actually met face-to-face with a person they had known only through the Internet (9 percent of thirteen- to fifteen-year-olds and 22 percent of sixteen- to seventeen-year-olds).
- 30 percent have considered meeting someone they've only communicated with online.
- 71 percent reported receiving messages online from someone they don't know.
- 45 percent have been asked for personal information by someone they don't know.
- When teens receive messages online from someone they don't know, 40 percent usually reply to and chat with that person.
- Only 18 percent said they tell a parent or guardian that they received a message from someone they don't know.

- 33 percent of thirteen- to seventeen-year-olds reported that their parents or guardians know "very little" or "nothing" about what they do on the Internet.
- 48 percent of sixteen- to seventeen-year-olds said their parents or guardians know "very little" or "nothing" about their online activities.
- Fully 22 percent of those surveyed reported their parents or guardians have never discussed Internet safety with them.

We need a new "don't talk to strangers" pep talk, and hopefully this book will help you start the conversation in your home.

We are so attentive in the early years to giving them the "don't talk to strangers" pep talk, but then we allow them to hang out with more than 990 million people who have access to the Internet!

The Need to Protect Them from Themselves

The preteen and teen years are often thought of as the conformity years. Our children will use these years to search for their identity and purpose in an attempt to find their place in the world. They will most often look to their friends for approval and acceptance. While in the process of finding their voice, many will make poor choices in a desperate attempt to fit in and be accepted. They live for the moment and rarely give a thought to the long-term consequences of an action. We preach to them about the dangers of alcohol, drugs, and sex outside of marriage and remind them of the consequences. It is not likely to sink in and act as a deterrent unless we talk about it over and over again. The same is true with technology.

Our kids have grown up alongside technology and have yet to hear the long-term horror stories that can result from using it irresponsibly and sharing too much information. Only recently are these stories beginning to surface in the news. It is no secret that many school officials, colleges, employers, and others are taking advantage of the bread-crumb trail our kids are leaving and doing extensive background checks. Our kids naively believe that their actions are private and that the average adult is incapable of penetrating their perceived private online worlds. In reality, every comment they make, every picture they post, and every step they take is forever saved and cached away even after they have deleted it. Eighty-one percent of parents and 79 percent of teens state that teenagers aren't careful enough when giving out information about themselves online. Sixty-five percent of parents and 64 percent of teens say that teenagers do things online that they wouldn't want their parents to know about.[3] One can only begin to imagine what the political mudslinging ads will look like in the years to come when this generation of youth begins to run for office! In future chapters we will address the issue of sharing too much information.

Our kids naively believe that their actions are private and that the average adult is incapable of penetrating their perceived online worlds.

First Things First

Before we dive into the book and begin to discuss the technology that impacts our children, let's begin with a few prerequisites. The first two are mandatory while the third one is optional (but strongly recommended).

1. First and Foremost a Commitment to Be Your Child's Parent

Perhaps one of the most shocking discoveries I made in the process of researching for this book was the comfort among many children/teens in typing things they would never say to someone's face. In addition, there seem to be no rules when it comes to uploading and posting pictures and videos to the Web. I will address the issue of picture and video uploading in chapter 5. Oftentimes, when I stumble upon such profiles (many of them church kids), I find myself wondering, *Where in the world are their parents?* I cannot tell you how many discussions I have had with parents who have no clue what their kids are posting online. I have met others who simply don't care. They would rather remain in good favor with their child (translation: be their buddy, ol' pal) than properly train them and draw boundaries (translation: be their God-ordained parent).

If you are a parent who makes a habit of uttering the phrase, "Ah, kids will be kids," on a recurring basis, do me a big favor. Close this book and pop yourself upside the head with it. Now open it back up and continue reading. Your child doesn't need another buddy; your child needs a parent. And let's not be fooled. Someday we will stand before God and be held accountable for the way we raised the children that were entrusted to us. That doesn't mean you can't be your child's friend, but you have to get it in the right order. Parent first, friend second.

2. An Open Mind

You've heard the proverbial saying, "Never say never." Well, it certainly applies to our attitudes when it comes to our children's participation in the ever-shifting landscape of technology. If you picked up this book with the mind-set that, "My child will never be allowed to IM/have a cell phone/get a MySpace or Facebook page/freely surf the Web," then I can almost assure you that this book will frustrate you. I did not write this book to point out the evils of technology and encourage you to ban your children from using it. I wrote this book as a fellow parent who after saying, "I will never . . ." on a few occasions, came to the conclusion that I was responding based on fear rather than trusting God for the answers.

God began gently to remind me that my responsibility as a parent was to prepare my children to live in the world without becoming "of the world." Romans 12:2 tells us, *"Don't copy the behavior and customs of this world, but let God transform you into a new person by changing the way you think. Then you will know what God wants you to do, and you will know how good and pleasing and perfect his will really is"* (NLT).

Some might interpret that verse to mean that we should join our Amish friends by abstaining from all technology since it could open a Pandora's box of worldly evils. I, however, am not willing to give up my cell phone, laptop, and iPod loaded chock-full of old eighties songs in the pursuit. The key will be finding balance by using technology in ways that are pleasing to God.

While many parents are understandably fearful of exposing their children to too much too soon, it is unreasonable to ban them completely from technology. By the time they leave the nest and enter the real world, they will be forced into an environment that assumes they have a basic knowledge of the latest technology. If we fail to offer them guidance along the way while they are under our roofs, we do them a disservice in the long run. Opinions differ concerning the appropriate age to begin IMing, to get a cell phone, to text message, or to participate in social networking sites. Once you have a better understanding of the pros and cons of each forum of communication, you will be better equipped to decide when your child is old enough to participate. Every child is different; and you, of course, know your child best.

3. Time

I'm sure you're probably wondering by now what is involved in staying engaged in your children's logged-on lives and, more importantly, how much time it will take out of your busy day. First, let me reassure you that you will not have to quit your day job. It will take some time, especially on the front end, as you learn how to spot-check your kids' activity; but once learned, it will become a standard part of your routine. Also, you only need one parent to take on the challenge. If you know right now your spouse would be better suited for this role, you might consider handing this book off to him or her.

Most parents have learned the art of checking the history on the computer to see where their children have been. I don't even bother to do this because I have monitoring software that does the job for me. Besides, most children know how to clear the history so you can't track the Web sites they've visited. The monitoring software I have sends an activity report straight to my inbox every hour on the hour. Assuming you choose the path of monitoring software and follow my advice of setting further boundaries by requiring your teen's passwords to any profiles they have set up on the Web, let me give you an idea of what an average spot-checking day looks like for a mother of two teens (my oldest is away at college, and I do not monitor his activity with software). Now, keep in mind that I write full-time; therefore, my laptop is always nearby. That said, I choose to check their activity on a daily basis. If you are not on your computer daily, you can monitor your children's activity on a weekly basis.

Each morning I check my e-mail and scan over one or more of the hourly reports detailing a list of sites visited by my children on the computers they use. Note: I do not go over them all, or it would consume my entire day. After scanning a report or two, I notice the typical sites my eighth-grade son enjoys: ESPN.com, addictinggames.com, aim.com (for AOL instant messenger). I then scroll through subject lines of IM conversations that have been e-mailed directly to my Inbox. I look specifically for new screen names or conversations with certain friends that have caused a flag in my spirit previously. I quickly scan over those messages, looking particularly for anything that would be dangerous or inappropriate. This would include suggestive statements, links to inappropriate Web sites, evidence of cyberbullying, or contact by a stranger. If I find something, I save the conversation to discuss later. If necessary, I ask my son or daughter to block the individual in the future.

After scanning over IM conversations, I then log onto MySpace and Facebook to check my children's pages. The monitoring software I use does not currently track specific comments and pictures on my children's pages, so my only means of monitoring is to go directly to their pages.

I do a quick scan on their profile pages, looking particularly for new comments posted by others on the page. I also check their pictures to make sure they have used good judgment on the photos uploaded to their pages. I also check to make sure they haven't added any information that could allow someone to track their steps (where they are going this weekend, etc.). As an extra-added bonus, I briefly scan my college-aged son's page. After a quick spot-check, I have a pretty good idea of what he's up to even though he is more than eight hundred miles away. This includes numerous girls who comment on his "wall." Who knows—one of these gals could be my future daughter-in-law! I am able to click through to see cute pictures of a sorority formal he attended, tailgate parties, and the like. It's a treat to get a glimpse of his new life away from home. Many parents of college kids, upon seeing their pages, might use the word *shock* rather than *treat*, so I feel especially blessed. After that, I am finished checking, and I move on to the rest of my busy day. All of the above can be done in about fifteen to thirty minutes, depending on how many IM conversations I choose to read. In the beginning, it took longer as I pored over the conversations to learn who was talking to my children and the overall content of their discussions. Once I got a good idea of their circle of friends, I learned the art of spot-checking.

After recovering from the initial shock that comes with the discovery that our wired teens are accustomed to sharing much more information than the average parent would feel comfortable with, I believe you will come to see some positives in the way they communicate today. Just as with most anything else, technology can be used for good or evil. Being a caring, engaged parent takes time. The truth is, many parents are running ragged with their own busy schedules; and rather than parent *proactively*, many parent *reactively* by running interference only after a problem arises. When it comes to our children's technology habits, too much is at stake simply to react when things go wrong or, worse, to tune out and fail to react at all. If we are to parent proactively, we must prioritize the time needed to help guide our kids along the way.

The truth is, many parents are running ragged with their own busy schedules; and rather than parent *proactively*, many parent *reactively* by running interference only after a problem arises.

A Word about Monitoring Software

While using monitoring software like the one I mentioned above is not required, it is highly recommended. Monitoring software actually tracks kids' every keystroke and takes screen shots (pictures) of their Internet activity. I find that most parents have installed some sort of safety filter (an absolute must), but few are familiar with monitoring software. They are not one in the same. I have both installed on my home computers in order to provide as many levels of protection as possible. The software I use was just under one hundred dollars and has no monthly payments. It has more than paid for itself. Not only is it more thorough than any other option I can find, but it also saves me the time of having to physically check the history on the computer each and every day. The main advantage is the ability to view your child's IM conversations, e-mails, and some (not all) postings made on blog sites. When checking the history on the computer, it will not give you logs of conversations but rather simply show you that they accessed instant messenger or their e-mail account. What they actually did beyond that will be a mystery.

Some monitoring software programming will not only record transcripts of IM conversations and e-mails sent and received but also e-mail the transcripts directly to your Inbox. While it might be tempting to read through their IM conversations in detail to get a better idea of what exactly is going on in their little heads, we must remember that the ultimate goal is not to stalk their every movement but rather to make sure they are using the technology responsibly. In addition to receiving transcripts of IM conversations, my monitoring software also e-mails me reports (daily) of exactly which sites have been accessed, what time they were accessed, and for how long. If I see sites that I am not familiar with or appear inappropriate, I click through to check them out further.

I should warn you that monitoring software is controversial, and many people are of the mind-set that it is an invasion of privacy. It always amazes me when doing radio and TV interviews and discussing monitoring software that some hosts will pose the question of whether or not I feel I am invading my kids' privacy by monitoring their online activity. My answer is always the same. "One in five kids ages ten to seventeen has been solicited for sex online, and one in thirty-three has been aggressively solicited where the predator attempted to set up a meeting with the child in person.[4] Law enforcement officers estimate that as many as fifty thousand sexual predators are on the Web at any given time."[5] Given that information, I point out that it is irresponsible for parents *not* to monitor where their kids are going online, who they are talking to, and what they are saying. And you can rest assured predators are trolling the Web at any given time and are more than happy to communicate with your child, especially if they sense the parents are absent or disengaged. A sobering thought, but in too many cases, an accurate one.

All three of my teens know that there is monitoring software installed on our home computers. My personal philosophy is that it is appropriate to tell your children that you will be monitoring their online activity. I do, however, have an exception to the rule. If a parent has a reason to believe that a child is involved in dangerous behaviors and further believes the child would try to cover his tracks if he knew he was being monitored, then it is more than fair not to tell him. An example would be a child that a parent suspects is drinking, doing drugs, or could be at risk for suicide. It is a parent's responsibility not only to intervene to protect the child from harming himself but to head the problem off at the pass before he harms others.

If that is not your situation and you plan to install monitoring software, the younger they are and the earlier you tell them, the better. My oldest son was about fourteen when I installed the monitoring software. When I informed him, he gave me the hardest time. He harassed me about it for several years and felt like I was spying on his every move. I continued to reassure him that while I trusted him, I did not necessarily trust others who were making contact with him from the outside. I further reminded him that I was only spot-checking from time to time and not stalking his every move. By the time he entered his senior year in high school, I no longer felt there was a need even to spot-check his online activity. He had his own laptop at that point and was preparing to leave for college, so it seemed like the right time to cut him loose.

His younger sister, on the other hand, was twelve when I installed the monitoring software. She was much more accepting of my explanation. Because I installed it at the front end of her Internet activity, she and her younger brother have known no other way of life. In fact, when she was about fourteen, I intercepted an IM conversation she was having with her older brother that caused me to laugh out loud. At the time, I was out of town at a book signing and sitting in the lobby of my hotel checking my e-mails. An IM transcript of her conversation with her brother landed in my Inbox. They were discussing a girl that my son had his eye on that just so happened to be a friend of my daughter's. Paige was informing my son Ryan that she had firsthand information about who this girl liked and said, "I will tell you who she likes, but you have to keep it between you and me." Following that statement, she added, "And mom cuz we know she's reading this." She then added, "Hi Mom." I literally laughed out loud.

I believe that our children, though they likely won't admit it, want us to be engaged in their lives and draw boundaries for their protection. I can't promise you that you'll get a shout-out from your child in an IM transcript that lands in your inbox, but I can promise you that you are doing the right thing by getting involved in your kids' wired worlds. (More information about monitoring software, including a link to the monitoring software I use can be found at www.loggedonandtunedout.com.

It's Time to Log On!

Now that we have set the groundwork and the troops have been rallied, it's time to dive in and tackle the great unknown. The following chapters will focus on their primary means of communication and hopefully will provide you with enough understanding to begin conversations with your children about using technology in a responsible manner. Note that this book is not a comprehensive approach to all media and does not address MP3 players, television, movies, online gaming, portable gaming devices, etc. Another book for another time. This book focuses on the technology that influences the way our children communicate with their peers and the outside world.

Some of the information you will read in the following chapters will stretch your understanding, but don't give up. Continue to remind yourself that if our kids can grasp the technology, surely we can too. I should also warn you that some of the information presented in the following chapters will shock you. Don't let that scare you away. Knowledge is power when it comes to helping our kids use technology responsibly. Most importantly, remember that God has provided us with everything we need to equip our children to use technology in a manner that would bring glory and honor to his name. It was never his intent to leave us without a game plan.

Knowledge is power when it comes to helping our kids use technology responsibly.

CHAPTER 2

Instant Messaging: The Party Never Ends

Most kids start clamoring for a screen name around the same time the begging and pleading for a cell phone begins. And trust me, that age keeps getting younger and younger. My college-age son didn't really pick up on IMing until late into his eighth-grade year. My daughter begged to IM with a few select friends in fifth grade. My younger son grew up watching the older two communicate back and forth with their friends through this medium. So I shouldn't have been the least bit surprised to discover that his older sister had helped him set up a screen name when he was in the third grade.

"DaBombHKC" was only allowed to IM his older sister or brother, so he officially had two buddies on his buddy list. After about one week the novelty wore off, and he was back to doing what third-grade little brothers do best . . . pester their older siblings. That is, until he hit the sixth grade and informed me that, "Evrrrreeeeeebody is allowed to IM" but him. So I agreed to a trial run by giving him some limited IMing privileges after his homework was done and before the dinner bell rang. By this time I had figured out enough about IMing to throw together a basic safety pep talk: "Never talk to strangers. Don't add 'friends of friends' to your buddy list. Never click through on links others may send to you. Never accept invitations to go to public chat rooms. Never type something you wouldn't say to someone face-to-face. And finally, never say anything that would bring dishonor to God's name."

In addition to having him sign off on the rules above, I also required him to place his fingers on the keyboard properly just as he would learn someday in a keyboarding class and told him that if I caught him with his fingers improperly placed, he would not be able to IM that day. I had implemented this silly little rule with his older two siblings, and as a result all three of my kids type faster than I could ever hope to do.

While monitoring my youngest son's IM activity, I discovered much to my pleasure that he was using technology in a responsible manner during this trial period. Unfortunately, I cannot say the same for a handful of other sixth graders who IMed him! Within a two-week period, he received an invitation from a classmate to visit a chat room that she claimed was "really funny." He did the right thing by declining, but the girl proceeded to cut and paste in detail some of the things that were being said in this chat room. By her description, it became clear that it was a masturbation chat room! Within days, a sixth-grade boy who is friends with my son IMed him and, in the course of conversation, made some joking references to oral sex.

Both of these children are from Christian homes and attend church regularly. In both situations my son did as I had told him and blocked the guilty parties from further conversation. I commended him for doing the right thing but explained that unfortunately his innocence had still been robbed. I further explained that because of the fact that some kids his age were not using IM in a positive manner, I could not risk it by continuing to allow him to IM. I told him that his father and I would re-evaluate the issue when he entered seventh grade. It is a shame that my son had to be penalized because of the irresponsibility of a couple of other kids.

We reinstated his IM privileges the following year, and amazingly most of the kids had done some growing up. Hayden knows that I am spot-checking his messages, and at times he will bring up conversations where other kids have used bad language or talked inappropriately. He recently transferred from private school to public school, and IMing friends has helped him gauge the character of potential new friends simply by examining how they behave on IM. One guy in particular drops the f-bomb rather frequently, and as a result Hayden has distanced himself from him. He admitted to me that it was obvious by carrying on IM conversations with this guy that he was not a good "weekend friend" candidate but rather someone who would fall into the "weekday friend" or "acquaintance" category. I share this to say that IMing can serve as a means for our children to do background or "character checks" among other students with whom they are communicating. I can preach to my kids about "choosing their friends wisely," but it is far more valuable when they can come to a logical conclusion on their own about the types of friends they desire to have.

I am certainly not suggesting that you help your eight-year-old set up a screen name and let her go to town with instant messenger. It will be up to you to decide when your child is ready to handle the responsibility of instant messaging. But remember, if you give it a try and discover as I did that it is too much, too soon, just step in and pull the plug. That's the great thing about being a parent. We can change our minds.

Instant messaging is the number one online activity for American girls eight to eighteen and number two online activity for boys. A marketing article addressing the online habits of teens notes that while many teens have their own cell phones, online communication reigns as the preferred method of chat. A Lycos survey showed that once the school day ends, 45 percent of teens preferred to communicate with their friends via IM outside of school while only 15 percent preferred to communicate face-to-face with their friends.[1] A Pew Internet researcher said that 68 percent of U.S. teens use instant messaging.[2] And in case you missed the memo, e-mail is so yesterday. Most teens maintain an e-mail account to receive attachments and communicate with teachers, relatives, and others who don't use IM. The general consensus among teens is that e-mail is for old people. (Translation: you and me!)

45 percent of teens preferred to communicate with their friends via IM outside of school while only 15 percent preferred to communicate face-to-face with their friends.

Think Before You Type!

When it comes to instant messaging, we need to be purposeful in teaching our kids to think before they type. They are more inclined to type things that they would never in a million years say to someone's face. I am shocked at the level of sexual banter that occurs through IMing. Ephesians 5:4 reminds us that obscenities, coarse joking, and foolish talk have no place among God's holy people. Fortunately, as more and more parents resort to monitoring software on their computers, word has begun to spread to preteen and teen users. This has acted as sort of a deterrent as many preteens and teens have become more careful about what they type, knowing that a parent is possibly reading the comments on the other end (if not their own parents!). Some of my kids' friends are aware that I monitor IMs sent or received from our home. One of my daughter's friends recently slipped and said a bad word in an IM conversation, only to follow it with "Whoops, I'm sorry Mrs. Courtney!" We also need to remind our kids that while their conversations might be "instant," they are also "permanent." Many are stored away on the hard drive, not to mention the person on the receiving end can save the messages. Just ask Congressman Mark Foley. Or should I say, ex-Congressman Foley? He resigned after copies of IM conversations he traded with a young Congressional page emerged in the news. Conversations, mind you, that occurred years prior but were stored away by the recipient. (Note: A comprehensive list of IM safety rules to go over with your children is included in the appendix.)

Old Habits Die Hard

Part of the convenience of IMing is that it is brief and to the point. The downside is that kids have created shortcuts when it comes to typing out words in an effort to communicate as quickly as possible. The same shortcuts used in IMing are also used in text messaging (next chapter). It's faster to say "brb" rather than "be right back." Many English teachers are saying that they are seeing this new "Webspeak" show up on school assignments. Stories are also emerging of this new shorthand showing up on SAT essays and college admission applications.

> **English teachers are saying that they are seeing this new "Webspeak" show up on school assignments.**

Want to get a laugh out of your kids? Insist that they can't IM unless they type out all the words and use proper punctuation. I actually tried implementing this rule out of a concern that their IM lingo would bleed over into their writing assignments at school. And I got what I deserved: treated as if I had just arrived from another planet. In fact, they still tease me about my attempt at the "IM grammar rule" to this day. Literally no one uses proper sentence structure and grammar when IMing, except for maybe old people like us. Just recently my daughter was at a friend's house and sent an IM to her younger brother that said, "What ya doin" (no punctuation). My husband was working on the computer when the message came through; and seeing that it was from Paige, he thought he'd play along and pretend to be her brother. He replied, "Nothing much. I am playing video games." Immediately, my daughter knew it wasn't her brother and replied, "Dad?" She had been tipped off by the presence of punctuation and use of full sentences.

About the only recourse we have is to make sure our children are in the habit of proofreading any written material, specifically looking for Webspeak that might show up accidentally before turning in assignments, job applications, etc. It might be a good idea for you to look over their papers in the beginning and point out anything they may have missed.

The Next Generation of Parenting

Several years ago I set up my own instant messenger account. I put my kids on my buddy list and a few friends who also had screen names and joined the world of instant messaging. From time to time, I sign on and have conversations with my kids who are sometimes in the next room! My daughter is not one to share her feelings much, and even though we are very close, it can be like pulling teeth to get her to open up. I have found that if I IM her when I notice that she is looking down and ask her how she's doing, amazingly, she will open up to me through this format. Again, it's easier to type things you might not be willing to say face-to-face, and as is true in this case, that also can be a positive.

If your children are IMing, I highly recommend that you set up your own screen name and put them on your buddy list. It's important that our children see that we are taking an active role in understanding the technology they use on a daily basis. If you're not sure how to set it up, ask your child. Again, this makes it more of a partnership and sends a clear message that Mom and Dad are stepping up to the plate. In addition, have the rule that you can spot-check their messages at any time and they are not allowed to "x out" of the screen if you approach them. (If you have monitoring software, this is not necessary but still a good rule to have on hand.) Below, you will find some common abbreviations used in IMing that will help you translate some of the messages you might see.

---

lol = laughing out loud

brb = be right back

btw = by the way

sup = what's up

idk = I don't know

ltr or l8r = later

otp = on the phone

yw = you're welcome

---

np = no problem

jk = just kidding

omg = oh my God/gosh (I'm not endorsing this slang, but this one is common.)

ttyl = talk to you later

thx = thanks

w/e = whatever

np = no problem

lylas = love ya like a sister

gtg = got to go

rents = parents

sys = see you soon

zzz = tired, bored

If your children are IMing, I highly recommend that you set up your own screen name and put them on your buddy list.

Here are some that could signal danger if you see them when spot-checking your child's IMs over their shoulder or scanning the IM transcripts sent by your monitoring software:

pos = parent over shoulder

mos = mom over shoulder

p911 = parent alert

paw = parents are watching

a/s/l = age, sex, location (often asked by
predators)

nifoc = naked in front of computer

420 = code for buying or smoking marijuana

In addition, remember these basic rules when IMing with your kids:

Don't type in all caps! It is considered yelling, and your child will think you are angry. Don't be guilty of poor netiquette!

Be brief. Much of the appeal of IMing with our kids is that it's short and sweet. Long conversations should be saved for face-to-face.

Don't blast them with back-to-back messages. Many times they are carrying on several conversations at one time, so be patient!

Don't nag them. Reminders to wear their retainer at night or take the garbage out are OK on occasion but should be used sparingly. Use the forum as a way to engage in fun conversation. If you use it primarily to parent them, it defeats the purpose.

Never IM their friends! Always let their friends IM you first if they are interested in talking. Some of my daughter's friends will ask for my screen name and IM me on occasion. Many will share their boy problems with me, and it has been such a wonderful opportunity to encourage them in the faith. Some are not Christians, and I have been able to broach the topic in many situations that would otherwise be awkward face-to-face with others present.

Always say good-bye. If you sign off abruptly without saying good-bye to those you've been talking to, it is the same thing as hanging up. No need to go into detail—just a brief "gtg make dinner! Bye!"

Now that my son has moved away to college (822 miles door-to-door!), I sign on to my instant messenger account several times a week. It has been an absolute joy to be able to stay in touch with him through this medium. And since many teens will stay signed on almost twenty-four hours a day and simply post an "away message" when they are away from their computers, I can sometimes keep track of what he's doing during the course of his day. A couple of weeks ago, I logged on, and his away message said "ultimate frisbee." I promptly sent him a message that said, "Your away message yesterday was 'guitar hero' and now it's 'ultimate frisbee' today. Are you studying? I'm worried about you, boy!" I think he's taken note that I'm checking the bread-crumb trail he's been leaving, because the last several times I've logged on, his away message has suspiciously said, "At the library." Yeah, right!

CHAPTER 3
Cell Phones: The Average Teen's Lifeline

Cell phones. We love them, and we hate them. They are easy to love when you find yourself on the side of the road with a flat tire or you're trying to track down your daughter and her friend after being separated while shopping in the mall. The love fades when the teenager sitting behind you at the movies won't hang up. Or even worse, one goes off in your purse right smack in the middle of a wedding (guilty as charged)!

The cell phone may be annoying at times, but I bet you can't imagine going a day without it.

If your child has one, he probably can't imagine going an hour without it. Such was the case with my fourteen-year-old son this past year. He accidentally left his phone behind while we were out of town for the weekend and had to live an entire week without it. You would have thought the boy had lost a limb or something. And in many ways, the cell phone has become like a necessary appendage to most teens. They don't leave home without it. It is their lifeline to the outside world.

"Friends" top a teen's list of priorities, and the cell phone is the glue that holds them together. Any parent who fails to realize the importance of a cell phone in a teen's life is completely out of touch with teens' logged-on lives. In fact, at a recent event for middle school and high school girls where I was the speaker, I asked girls to think about what one item they would take with them if they were going to spend time on a deserted island. The majority chose their cell phones. It beat out the iPod, laptop computer, and, unfortunately, even their Bible.

About sixteen million teens and younger kids have cell phones, with the bulk of them being older teens, according to the researcher GFK's NOP World Technology. That adds up to about 60 percent of all teens, and each year the age of ownership gets younger. Even Disney has jumped into the cell phone craze, offering a line of kid-friendly phones complete with GPS tracking devices to help parents pinpoint their child's location. In New Zealand 84 percent of children have a cell phone by the age of fourteen. Harris Interactive data from 2006 shows that 23 percent of children ages eight to twelve own a mobile phone, up from 12 percent the previous year.

As a parent who swore, "My kids will never have a cell phone until high school," I have had to eat my words with my last two children. And I must admit, it was worth it for the peace of mind in knowing I could reach them when I needed to. I am every bit as dependent on their having phones as they are. Gone are the days where our parents loaded us up with quarters when we headed out the door. You would be hard-pressed even to find a pay phone these days. Most have been retired to the nearest landfill. In a recent report, among those in the U.S. who own mobile phones, 74 percent say they have used their handheld device in an emergency and gained valuable help.[1] Clearly, this is a major factor for many parents when considering whether or not the pros outweigh the cons when it comes to purchasing a cell phone for their children.

And why wouldn't tweens and teens beg for a cell phone. Most of the phones they are clamoring for come equipped with games, text messaging, a camera for pictures and video clips, Internet access, MP3 player, alarm clock, address book, calendar, and other teen-friendly features. The cell phone has replaced the home phone, and most teens couldn't recite their top three friends' home digits if you offered them a cash prize. Their cell phone is their mobile "friend list" and keeps them in touch around the clock with their top one hundred friends. Just recently my daughter's cousin who lives out of town sent her a text saying she had just gotten a new car. Following the text came a picture of the car. This reminded me of a recent shopping trip where my daughter and her friend split off to look for a new pair of jeans. I told my daughter that I wanted to see them before she bought them, and a half hour later my phone vibrated (ever since the wedding debacle, my phone is always set on the vibrate feature!). She sent me a text message telling me what store she was in and followed with several pictures of her posing in the jeans straight from the dressing room. Interesting. And it's reasons like this that the teens love their cell phones.

Most parents are familiar with cell phones and have a vague awareness of the features they offer.

Below, I will give a brief overview of some of the popular features and address the primary concerns. It will be up to you, the parent, to decide what age is appropriate for your child to have a cell phone and which features you deem allowable. If you don't feel your child can be responsible with some of the features, either find a phone with the basics or deactivate the features in question.

The cell phone has replaced the home phone, and most teens couldn't recite their top three friends' home digits if you offered them a cash prize.

Talking

Most teens become well versed in the peak/off-peak hours of their provider in order to maximize their talk time. Usually this comes as a result of being grounded a time or two after Mom and Dad see the monthly phone bill. Since most providers offer off-peak hours in the evenings, parents should be clear on any curfews that are in order. Since our teens are no longer tethered to a corded phone in the family room, parents are out of the loop on who is calling and when the calls occur. Since the ringers on phones can be silenced, they can literally talk the night away. Remember though, you are the parent, and you can draw up the rules any way you want. Some parents confiscate the phone in the evenings (especially if the child is younger) and give it back in the morning.

Another often overlooked issue among young cell phone users is the lack of etiquette. Who among us has not experienced the misfortune of being trapped in an enclosed space with an oblivious cell phone yacker? In a recent study, 82 percent of all Americans and 86 percent of cell users report being irritated at least occasionally by loud and annoying cell users who conduct their calls in public places.[2] Who are these rude people? Could it be your children? Could it be you? It's possible. The same study found that nearly one in ten cell phone owners (8 percent) admitted they themselves have drawn criticism or irritated stares from others when they are using their cell phones in public.[3]

> **In a recent study, 82 percent of all Americans and 86 percent of cell users report being irritated at least occasionally by loud and annoying cell users who conduct their calls in public places.**

Parents need to spend time going over cell phone etiquette with their children and have consequences for bad cell phone manners. In the appendix, I have included a quiz you can go over with your child to see where she ranks when it comes to cell phone etiquette. Was that your daughter who was yacking away in the stall next to me in the airport restroom last week? I hope not! Enough is enough. Parents need to make sure their kids know when it's appropriate to pick up and when it's appropriate to hang up.

Texting

Americans sent nearly sixty-five billion text messages in the first six months of 2006, nearly double the number sent during the same period the year before.[4] A recent survey found that 80 percent of Americans ages eighteen to twenty-nine own cell phones, and 65 percent of those text message on a regular basis. After talking, texting is the most important function people are looking for in their cell phones, says Miro Kazakoff, head of the handset research practice at Boston-based Compete, Inc. More important than the camera. More important than Bluetooth.[5]

Most cell phone companies offer text-messaging packages that give teens incentive to text rather than talk. It is similar to instant messaging in that it provides the ability to cut to the chase when having a conversation rather than getting trapped in a lengthy conversation on the phone. However, parents should explain to their children that text messaging is not an acceptable forum for discussing more serious matters. Someone failed to mention that one to Britney Spears—who sent a text message to her then husband Kevin Federline, letting him know that she was divorcing him. Technology has enabled our teens to come out of their shells and express things they would otherwise struggle to say to someone face-to-face. However, that can be a good thing and a bad thing. They need to learn the proper balance and rules of etiquette.

Unfortunately, it is difficult for parents to monitor incoming and outgoing text messages, just short of snatching the cell phone off your child's nightstand when she is in the shower. You can let her know that you will be doing occasional spot-checks, but if she has something to hide, she will likely delete the messages in question. If you don't feel that your child is ready to use text messaging in a responsible manner, then don't add it to your service plan.

Just as I recommended in the previous chapter that you consider setting up a screen name in order to IM your children, I also recommend that you learn the art of text messaging in order to communicate with your child in this forum. In fact, almost 70 percent of all parents today are texters, according to the Pew Internet and American Life Project.[6] It is a wonderful way to let your child know you are praying for her before a test or to send her a reminder of your love. My daughter loves getting text messages from her dad, and one day a friend was with her when she received one that said "I luv u." Her friend responded with, "Ah, that is soooooo cute. I wish my dad would do that."

Instant Messaging

On a recent family vacation I was awakened by an annoying chiming sound in the wee hours of the morning. I traced it to my daughter's cell phone on the nightstand beside her bed. Unbeknownst to me, she had posted the following away message on her instant messenger account on our home computer. "Woo-hoo! On vacation at the beach! IM me!" She had programmed the IM messages she received to go straight to her cell phone as text messages. We had left the computer behind, but it still managed to follow us 750 miles across three state lines. Lovely. What about the word *vacation* did she not understand?

Parents need to be aware that most cell phones come equipped with the ability to have IMs sent to their computers forwarded directly to their phones, if they activate this feature. Again, if you are not comfortable with this, simply deactivate the feature or tell your child it is not allowed.

Parents need to be aware that most cell phones come equipped with the ability to have IMs sent to their computers forwarded directly to their phones, if they activate this feature.

Mobile Web

According to a Pew study, a quarter of teen cell phone users access the Web on their phones.[7] The

Wall Street Journal reported that Web sites intended for cell phones are even harder to filter than regular Internet pages.[8]

Many of the cell phones offered on the market today come equipped with wireless Internet capabilities, which allow children access to the Web, instant messaging capabilities, as well as the ability to download games that are not subject to the rating system. Every parent needs to ask plenty of questions on the front end prior to purchasing a phone, or you should become familiar with the features on your child's phone if you have already bought one. Many features have to be added to the plan, so this offers parents an added level of control. Others will show up on the bill as an extra charge, so make sure you are clear with your child from the beginning what is and is not allowed.

Pictures and Streaming Video

A camera feature becomes standard on many cell phones sold today. If your child's phone has this feature, make sure you discuss the information presented in chapter 5 regarding picture and video uploading. The same rules that apply to the Web also apply to taking, sending, and receiving pictures and videos on cell phones. One police detective in Louisville, Kentucky, had this to say: "A lot of the cases that were coming out, some of them were of males taking pictures of their genitals and sending those images out." He went on to say that most of the time the pictures were taken as a practical joke with someone else's camera phone. The article went on to state that the Metro Crimes Against Children Unit did not think it was a laughing matter and commented that "the person taking the picture, it's his own body part, it's still child pornography. They're producing it, they're distributing, they're in possession of it, and those are all felonies." The article further said that they had arrested five teens between the ages of twelve and sixteen in a four-month period and that the parents "were floored" and "didn't have a clue what was going on."[9]

Driving Hazards

Another valuable conversation to have with your child is that it is never acceptable to talk or text while driving. More than a quarter of cell phone owners (28 percent) admit they sometimes do not drive as safely as they should while they use their mobile devices.[10]

More than a quarter of cell phone owners (28 percent) admit they sometimes do not drive as safely as they should while they use their mobile devices.

More and more fatalities are ocurring as a result of distracted drivers who are on their phones. Many states have passed laws to make it illegal to talk on a cell phone while driving, while other states have proposed the legislation.

I have been firm with my kids about driving while talking or texting on their phones and threatened to take them up if I ever discover they have broken the rule. However, I have a confession to make. During the course of writing this book, my daughter had an accident while talking on her cell phone . . . to me! She was running late to a dentist appointment and got lost on the way. She called me to get directions, and in an effort to get her there on time, I began giving her directions while she drove. It was a rainy day, and the roads were wet. When she switched into the left lane to turn around after missing her turn, she cut off another car. It was heart-stopping to hear the crunch of metal and my daughter scream, "I hit a car!" Fortunately, no one was hurt, but both cars suffered damage. It was a painful lesson to both of us that exceptions should never be made to this rule. Nothing is worth the risk, including being late to a dentist appointment. I should have insisted that she pull over to the side of the road or safely into a parking lot to get the directions. I have since apologized to my daughter for my wrongdoing in the matter and emphasized our new "zero-tolerance" policy. I also went out and purchased her a hands-free headset and insisted that she put it on right after she buckles up and place her phone in her lap. If she has an emergency, she will have her phone nearby.

Cell phones are already a permanent fixture in our lives. In fact, in the near future, look for new cell phone models that consolidate all the teen favorites into one place. Teens will use their phones to talk, text, receive IMs being sent to their computers, access their music library, surf the Web, check their MySpace and Facebook pages, and even post comments and upload pictures and video clips straight to the sites from their phones. Much of the above is already possible, but in the near future it will become the standard. Keep that in mind when reading the remaining chapters on social networking sites and picture and video uploading. When it comes to being portable and communicating on the run, the cell phone is the central piece of technology that connects teens to their favorite activities. Best of all, it can fit in their back pocket. No wonder our kids are begging for one.

CHAPTER 4

Social Networking Sites: The Virtual Malt Shop

From malt shops in the fifties to roller rinks in the seventies, every generation of teenagers has gravitated to a place they can call their own. A place absent of rules, responsibilities, and, most importantly, parents. When I was in high school, the designated hangout was the local Sonic drive-in. On any given Friday night, you were almost guaranteed to find me circling through the Sonic with a carload of girlfriends in my baby blue Buick Regal. Our sole mission was to secure a coveted and extremely rare parking space. Adults knew better than to show up at the Sonic after 9:00 p.m. Besides, few were willing to wait in the long convoy of cars lined up in the left-turn lane waiting for their turn to circle through the restaurant. Sometimes the wait could be a half hour or more, but we often walked up and down the line of cars and visited with friends. My carload of friends almost always succeeded in flirting our way into a spot, especially if my amply bosomed friend Karen came along (just being honest here). And why was it so important to get a spot? Those who managed to snag a parking space were front row and center stage to the teen drama of MacArthur High School. The breakups, cat fights, and secret confessions kept us coming back week after week. And best of all, you could enjoy it with a cherry limeade and Tater Tots with cheese!

Today's teens have traded an empty parking space at the Sonic for prime real estate in cyberspace. With social networking sites such as MySpace and Facebook, everyone is guaranteed a spot, and the drive-thru is open twenty-four hours a day. There is no curfew, few rules, and for the most part, no adult chaperones. And trust me, this is one big drive-thru! Social networking sites allow users to create profiles, share pictures and video clips, and swap messages with an online network of friends. More than half (55 percent) of all online American teens ages twelve to seventeen use online social networking sites, according to a new national survey of teenagers conducted by the Pew Internet and American Life Project. The study found that 58 percent of girls and 51 percent of boys in the twelve to seventeen age group had created an online profile. Among those in the fifteen- to seventeen-year-old range, 70 percent of girls had online profiles compared with 57 percent of boys. Among those who use the sites, 91 percent of all social networking teens say they use the sites to stay in touch with friends they see frequently while 82 percent use the sites to stay in touch with friends they rarely see in person.[1] But perhaps the finding that most indicates the reigning importance of social networking sites in the lives of our teens is that 48 percent of teens who have profiles on social networking sites visit the sites one or more times a day. And remember, these sites are still in their infancy, so we can expect these statistics to increase over the years.

More than half (55 percent) of all online American teens ages twelve to seventeen use online social networking sites.

While there are many social networking sites on the Web, I will focus primarily on MySpace and Facebook since they have attracted the largest audience of teens. In the Pew Internet Research study that I mentioned previously, 85 percent of the social networking teens identified in the study said they maintain a profile on MySpace; coming in second is FaceBook with only 7 percent.[2] Of course, as fickle as teens can be, there just may be a new and better online hangout by the time you read this. However, be assured that social networking sites, regardless of the addresses, are here to stay. If there is a new and better site by the time you read this, the information provided in this chapter should still give you a general idea of what you would find on a social networking site. Unfortunately most parents have a negative view of social networking sites in light of media accounts that have focused on predators using the sites to contact children. While this is a valid concern, new studies are indicating that most teens are using the sites responsibly. We will discuss the safety of the sites in more detail later in this chapter.

MySpace was not the first social networking sight on the scene, but it has definitely been the most popular to date. It touts itself as "an online community that lets you meet your friends' friends," stating that it is for "everyone," including:

- Friends who want to talk online
- Single people who want to meet other singles
- Matchmakers who want to connect their friends with other friends
- Families who want to keep in touch; map your Family Tree
- Business people and coworkers interested in networking
- Classmates and study partners
- Anyone looking for long lost friends[3]

The second most popular social networking site is Facebook, which originally gained popularity as a network for college students and has since opened to the public. The description provided on the actual site is this: "Facebook is a social utility that helps people better understand the world around them. Facebook develops technologies that facilitate the spread of information through social networks, allowing people to share information online the same way they do in the real world. Facebook is made up of many networks—individual schools, companies or regions—each of which is independent and closed off to nonaffiliated users. To join Facebook, people can authenticate into a school or work network, or they can join a regional network. They can then create profiles to connect with friends, share interests, join groups, send messages, write notes, and post photos."[4]

"Facebook launched in February 2004, and the Web site now has more than thirteen million registered users across more than forty thousand regional, work, college, and high school networks. According to comScore, Facebook is the seventh most trafficked site on the Web and is the number one photo-sharing site."[5]

MySpace and Facebook vary slightly in what they offer, but overall, they implement the same concept of offering an online hangout to network socially. The best way to familiarize yourself with the sites is to access them. Facebook offers a "take a tour" feature that will give you a crash course tutorial on what an average page looks like. However, it will be impossible to view an actual page unless you set up an account. Even then, you are only able to view profiles of people who accept you as a friend. MySpace is easier to access a sample profile because many profiles are open to the public. However, should you go onto the site and stumble upon a profile that is less than wholesome, keep in mind that most teens never venture out of their immediate friend network. Once they set up their profile, their time and attention are focused on their own page and network of friends. In the meantime, I will provide you with a summary of the main features you can expect to find on a typical MySpace or Facebook page and give you the pros and cons of each site.

The Basics

The teen years have always been marked as the phase in life where self-absorption is at an all-time high. Try as they may (and most don't even try), it is difficult for teens to see past their own needs and desires. They are seeking identity and purpose. As they struggle to define who they are and what their place is in the world, they look to others for validation. It should come as no surprise that teens would be attracted to the social networking sites as a means to express themselves and find their voices. It offers the perfect platform for putting it all out there and boldly proclaiming, "This is who I am; take it or leave it." It's an opportunity to cultivate the narcissist within. Truth be told, we all have a deep desire for others to *know* us and, furthermore, for others to come away *liking* us. Setting up a profile on a social networking site helps satisfy the urge to feel connected to others.

It's All about Me, Myself, and I

A main portion of the "profile" will be the "about me" section, and users can decide how much or how little to include. It has a place for a profile picture, which will be the main picture on their site. Anytime they post a comment on another person's page, join a group, or are added on someone else's friend list, a thumbnail of the picture will appear with their display name beside it (which can be just about anything!). Their profile picture can be changed as often as they desire and be as common as a simple head and shoulders shot or something as random as a close-up of a street sign. My college-age son used a head shot of Ronald Reagan for a period of time, and my daughter used a shot of herself and a friend doing a Superman jump from one bed to another in a hotel room. Pretty much anything goes, and as long as the picture is stored somewhere on their computer (including older pictures which can be scanned), it can be uploaded to their page.

After adding a profile picture, the real fun begins. This is where users are given the option to fill in basic contact information such as e-mail address, screen name, cell phone, address, city, state, etc. Facebook provides an option for students to fill in their dorm/apartment name and class schedule (for the purpose of finding other students in your dorm or classes). Both sites also give users the option to post information about their favorite music, television shows, movies, books, hobbies, activities, heroes, and quotes.

My oldest son has listed the following under "interests" on his Facebook page:

> *God, Auburn, college football, Astros base-ball, UT basketball, music, TV, video games, conservatism, racquetball, ultimate Frisbee, Ronald Reagan*

> *Among his favorite quotes, he cites Ronald Reagan (do you get the sense he likes Reagan?), Benjamin Franklin, C. S. Lewis, and several from the hit show, The Office. My daughter lists her favorite Scripture verse (Jer. 29:11), quotes from a few of her friends, and the familiar quote from Eleanor Roosevelt, "No one can make you feel inferior without your consent."*

MySpace gives the option of filling in personal information such as status (married, single, etc.), why they are on the site (here for friends, dating, net-working, etc.), sexual orientation (straight, gay, bi, etc.), body type (height), ethnicity, religion, zodiac sign, smoke/drink (yes or no), children, education (including all schools attended), occupation, and income. Again, it is up to the person setting up the page to decide how much, if any, of the information they choose to post. In addition to answering the standard default questions above, some will choose to add a more personal account of who they are.

Here is an actual example I found on a fourteen-year-old girl's MySpace page:

About me:

My name is megen

I love to go to the mall

I love BBQ

I have a dog named poogie

I have two brothers

my friends are the best you'll ever find, so be
     jealous

unicorns are real animals

I hate girls that think they're cool because
     they wear hollister everyday

american eagle is way better than hollister anyday

I love jim carrey, ben stiller, and owen wilson

my two fave movies are zoolander and dumb
  and dumber

the second dumb and dumber was just stupid,
  but it is still very fun to quote

every Thursday night I watch the office, it is
  awesome

I want a digital camera

superman is my whole life

I hate leggings

the orange ninja turtle is the best

I was born on easter morning

I love my brothers to death, never ask me to
  pick a favorite, that's just retarded

I love blankets

I hate candy corn

I love candy canes

I have an awesome trampoline that's like
  super ghetto

soup is yucky, so is gravy

I cry in every movie, I cried in zoolander

I love christmas trees

my ipod=love

I am in choir, but I will never sing alone for anyone

pluto is still a planet in my heart

I hate thunderstorms, they scare me

Pros: Viewing a child's social networking site offers parents a window into the heart and soul of their child. The exercise of filling out the "about me" portion also provides a chance for teens to analyze their likes and dislikes and put them into words.

Viewing a child's social networking site offers parents a window into the heart and soul of their child.

Cons: It also offers a window into the heart and soul of the child to *others*. Unless privacy controls are used in order to keep strangers out and Mom and Dad check the page on a regular basis to ensure that their children are not sharing too much information, it can be an extremely dangerous forum. Even with privacy controls in place, our children should be taught that "less is always best." Discourage your teens from filling out surveys that ask personal and graphic questions and posting them to their page. The surveys are popular with girls, but most reveal far too much information.

Picture Perfect?

Pictures are a huge part of an average page on a social networking site, and digital cameras have made it possible to take hundreds of pictures and upload them immediately to the Web. In fact, most teens don't even bother to have their pictures developed. They simply set up multiple albums on the Web in order to share them with their friends. Friends are able to comment on individual pictures and share their thoughts. It is similar to putting together an actual album and handing it to a friend to view. Part of the joy is hearing the response from others as they view the album. It is the same concept on the social networking sites, except it is possible to share your album with everyone on your friend list or the general public if your page is not set to private. The topic of uploading pictures and videos to the Web is so important that it merits an entire chapter. The pros and cons will be addressed at length in chapter 5.

Dear Diary—An Open Book to Our Kids' Thoughts and Feelings

Another key feature of the social networking sites is the ability to blog (short for Weblog). The best way to describe a blog is to imagine the ability to post journal entries as often as you like, straight to your page. The main difference here is that you can send a bulletin to your friends notifying them every time you post a new entry (blog). They can read your blog postings and comment on it if they choose. Teens write about a vast array of topics, ranging from deep ponderings of their soul to the absurd. I have read blog entries about meaningful mission trips, annoying parents, the frustrations of being grounded, books that inspire, poetry written from the heart, and the list goes on. Imagine what can happen when a platform is provided to post your free-flowing thoughts for the viewing pleasure of others and receive their immediate feedback.

Many teens choose not to use the blog feature at all (typically, the ones who don't enjoy journaling/writing). Yet others find it a benefit to participating in the social networking sites. Some use it as a forum to discuss ideas with their peers. For example, my son does not enjoy journaling, but he recently posted a note (blog) to his Facebook page asking his friends to weigh in on whether or not he should use his birthday money to buy a Nintendo Wii or an X-box 360. About ten of his friends posted their opinions on his page within a twenty-four-hour period. This served to be much more efficient than calling his friends one by one to ask them which system (if any) they owned and the pros and cons of each one.

<u>Pros:</u> Anytime we can get our kids to write constructively, it is a good thing. However, on the social networking sites, they need to limit their audience to real-life friends and be careful not to share too much information. General observations about their world, their faith, and poetry might be acceptable, but make sure they are not using the blog to purge their every thought and feeling by discussing their breakups, enemies, annoyances, or other information that involves others. Many parents have been alerted to personal struggles their children are having by reading their blog.

Many parents have been alerted to personal struggles their children are having by reading their blog.

<u>Cons:</u> It's hard to come up with hard and fast rules about what is acceptable to write about and what isn't. While it can be therapeutic for teens to purge their feelings, it can have long-term consequences if they fail to use good judgment about what

is acceptable reading for others. Some things are better suited to remain in a private diary or journal.

Meet My Three Hundred New Best Friends

It used to be common back when I was a teen to collect stamps, coins, or autographs of sport's players. Today's teens collect friends. And some have hundreds, many of whom they have never met face-to-face and probably never will. It's called "friending," and the social networking sites have made it possible. The qualifications to be someone's friend on MySpace or Facebook are determined by the user. Some accept total strangers who send a request their way while others require a simple qualifying connector (he's in my biology class; she's my best friend's sister, etc.), and yet others are more picky and limit their friend list to their inner circle of friends. Most teens opt for the simple qualifying connector in order to build a robust friend list without looking desperate to the point of accepting just anyone. Parry Aftab, an expert on teen safety and the Internet, says, "Friending is a way of finding status and is the definition of who you are online. You are judged by your friend list." And Susan Lipkins, an adolescent psychologist in Port Washington, New York, says, "If you go to college and you don't have a full bunch of people on your MySpace or Facebook, then it's implying that there's something wrong with you. Listing your buddies and your friends is a way of establishing yourself, of feeling connected and feeling like you're accepted."[6]

Parry Aftab, an expert on teen safety and the Internet, says, "Friending is a way of finding status and is the definition of who you are online. You are judged by your friend list."

Some teens feel obligated to accept anyone and everyone who sends them a friend request for fear they will eventually find out if they decline them. The sites do not notify users of declined friend invitations, so it is not likely unless someone is keeping track of their requests. Even so, this is a source of tension for many teens. The etiquette for requesting friends is still evolving, and you will get many opinions. My college-age son, for example, recently told me that he finds it annoying when people he hardly knew in high school send him friend requests as a means to "stay in touch" now that they are away at college. He is rather logical and doesn't see why they would be interested in staying in touch now when they hardly spoke while attending the same school together for four years. My daughter, on the other hand, welcomed the idea of staying in touch with students from her private school when she transferred to a public high school, even if it was someone she didn't know very well beforehand.

MySpace offers the added feature of sorting your favorite friends into a top four, top eight, top twelve, or top sixteen category that appears at the top of your friend list. And imagine the girl drama that occurs when someone is listed in one person's "top eight" friend list and it's not reciprocated. I single out the girls because the guys tend not to get as stressed over such details as not being included in someone's "top eight" friends. It is no different from the raw emotion we may have felt as a teen upon discovering that one of our friends was having a certain number of girls over and we didn't make the cut. Yet today it is played out daily. It is not uncommon for girls to guilt their friends over not being listed in their top group of friends. Some people find it so stressful that they opt instead to have their friends listed in random order (an option that is available for the faint at heart).

Pros: Having a way to stay in touch with friends even after they move away to college or graduate school is wonderful. My son has been able to stay in touch with friends from his high school or at least the ones who mattered most.

Cons: Many friend lists are too large and need to be cleaned up. It is hard for teens to say no to friend requests; therefore many are littered with acquaintances rather than true friends. Some students will build large friend lists as a result of poor self-esteem.

It is hard for teens to say no to friend requests; therefore many are littered with acquaintances rather than true friends.

If You Love Me, You'll Post on My Wall

Do you remember the thrill of getting your yearbook signed at the end of the school year? I know for girls it was common to rush home, close ourselves up in our bedrooms, and pore over each and every hand-scrawled note. What did our crush say? Did our best friend fill up an entire page? Who said we were cute? Funny? A blast to be around? And most importantly, how many signatures did we get? To have pages and pages of signatures sent a signal that we were liked. It served as a boost to self-esteem and tangible proof that we mattered.

Believe it or not, many students today don't even bother to have their yearbooks signed at the end of the year. And why would they? This generation of teens receives written kudos on a daily basis from their peers. The social networking sites provide a forum for friends to send comments that are then posted on the user's page (Facebook calls it a "wall"). Users have the option of preapproving the comments before they appear on their page, which I highly recommend in an attempt to weed out crude comments. Not that it seems to matter to some students who appear to have no moral compass and, therefore, approve anything sent their way, perhaps in a desperate attempt to log as many wall posts as possible. Wall posts are typically sent by the user's inner circle of online friends and can serve as a good gauge of the kind of company the person keeps.

A sampling of comments appearing on my daughter's Facebook wall today include:

i love you paigey! it was great seeing you
today :)

PAiGE! POR QUE? OKAY WELL THE REAL
REASON i'M WRiTiNG ON YOUR WALL
iS TO TELL YOU THAT i AM iNCREDiBLY
SORRY BECAUSE i ACCiDENTALLY WORE
YOUR SHOES HOME...

paige youre beautiful. i miss you haha

you are to cute for words paigey! i miss you.
we need to hang out soon now that i actually have a car :)

Paige i hope you feel better so we can hang
out soon!!

i love you and i am on the phone with you
right now

Paige . . . we are hanging out SOON. like
seriously . . . oh and i'm so excited that
you are going on the spring break mission
trip :)

You get the picture. It's "yearbook signing day"
every day on the sites! What person (especially
girl) wouldn't like being reminded on a consistent
basis of how much they are loved by their closest
friends?

Wall posts do not appear to take the place of face-to-face interaction, but rather accentuate already established relationships. They serve as a means to touch base with someone or simply drop in and say hello. People use them to have mini conversations about any and everything. Some argue that it detracts from face-to-face communication, but in reality these are the types of conversations that we used to have on the telephone. The drawback, of course, is that others can "listen in" just by reading the wall. One friend of mine found out that her daughter's new digital camera had been stolen when she read a comment on her daughter's wall that said, "Have you told your mom about your camera yet?" Teens use it as a means to converse back and forth and never imagine that anyone undesirable (to them) would read the comments (this includes us!). They discuss the upcoming party and discuss the details after the party. It's not uncommon to see comments like "Wow, you were pretty wasted last night. How are you feeling today?" Again, they never imagine that their perceived private online world can be penetrated by some in the adult population. By monitoring the comments posted on my daughter's Facebook wall, I have been able to call gently some things to her attention that she otherwise would have failed to see. One time she received a wall post from a friend in one of her classes who made a sarcastic remark about their teacher. I pointed out to my daughter that many school officials and teachers have access to the sites through student interns and that her teacher could possibly see the comments. She removed the comment, but it was clear by her reaction that the thought had never occurred to her before.

Pros: Wall posts can offer a temporary boost in self-confidence and remind teens that they matter to others. Many people have a hard time complimenting others face-to-face but won't hesitate to do so on someone's page/wall.

Cons: Due to the unpredictability of others, wall posts can sometimes be graphic and inappropriate. MySpace allows preapproval of comments, and Facebook has an option to delete comments after they appear.

E-mail Is So Yesterday

Another feature on the social networking sites is the ability to send a private message to another user. Because teens are in the habit of checking their page at least once a day, other teens use the messaging feature as a means to reach them. Teens consider e-mail a thing of the past and don't check it as often as they do their social networking pages. The messaging feature is similar to e-mail; and when users log onto their page, it notifies them of messages received. It is different from wall posts in that the comments are not posted publicly on the page/wall and are only viewable by the person they are sent to (and those standing over their shoulder!). Just as we experience the excitement of getting snail mail or e-mail from friends, teens like to log on and see that they have multitudes of messages in their in-boxes.

Teens consider e-mail a thing of the past and don't check it as often as they do their social networking pages.

Pros: Messaging offers a way to swap more personal messages without having to post publicly to a friend's page or wall.

Cons: Just as with e-mail and IMing, we will need to remind our children that even their messages sent in this format are not private. They should always assume that others could be standing over the recipient's shoulder. Also, comments once sent are saved in the recipient's in-box until they choose to delete them. If they are sending something they would not want someone to have a record of later on, it's best to say it rather than send it.

If they are sending something they would not want someone to have a record of later on, it's best to say it rather than send it.

Join the Club

The social networking sites also allow their members to create or join groups. MySpace offers everything from "The Jesus loving church of MySpace" to the "I believe in alien abductions." Teens tend not to participate in many groups on MySpace, but Facebook is another story. Just like on MySpace, groups vary from deep and thoughtful to outrageous and wacky. Creating or joining a group can provide a means for teens to identify with a cause or common interest. I often tell parents that they can learn more about a teen by viewing their list of Facebook groups. A sampling of the groups listed on my daughter's page are:

- Cheerleading is a sport
- I think High School Musical is better than real life
- Young people waiting for marriage
- When I was your age, Pluto was a planet
- We miss Lauren Andrews Brown (a memorial site for a family friend who passed away)

Some of my son's groups include:
- Auburn Christians
- Pro-life
- Animals were made for eating
- If my American flag offends you then leave my country

Anyone with a cause can start a group, and most groups are open to the Facebook public to join. Users can enter words in a group search engine to see if a group exists that matches their preference. For example, if you are hopelessly addicted to Starbucks Grande Vanilla Lattes (like I am!), you can enter "Starbucks" into the search engine, and a list of groups that have already been started will appear. If you don't find one that suits your needs, you can create the group, write up a description, appoint yourself an officer, and send out an invitation to anyone (or everyone) on your friend list to join. There is even a place for members to post comments on the group "wall."

"Today, at the age of 16 or 17, you can create a movement," says Ginger Thomson, CEO of YouthNoise, an online site created to help teens find and act on social causes. Thomson says it's only a matter of time before young people transform the Internet into an even more powerful force. The article goes on to list the "Top 10 advocacy groups on Facebook." They are as follows:[7]

Group	Members
1. Reduce the Drinking Age to 18!	111,275
2. Legalize Same-Sex Marriage	80,458
3. Americans for Alternative Energy	69,465
4. Support a Woman's Right to Choose	66,806
5. Support Stem Cell Research	55,219
6. Abolish Abstinence Only Sex Education	54,712
7. Government + Religion = Disaster	47,949
8. AIDS / HIV research	24,789
9. Equal Rights for Gays	24,013
10. Pro-Life	22,409

Again, groups range from the serious to the random, but the goal is the same: a gathering place for people who share the same beliefs or goals as other members in the group. Never before have teens and college students been given such a collective voice for a cause. Take for example one group I stumbled upon that literally made me laugh out loud. Boasting more than 20,000 members, the group "I'm Saving Myself for Wild, Passionate, Awkward Honeymoon Sex" has encouraged those committed to abstinence that they are not alone. In addition to finding many positive groups, I was also disturbed to find an abundance of inappropriate groups and many with a large number of members. Everything from "drink all you can now because when you're older it's called being an alcoholic" to "I'm not a slut; I'm just sexually popular."

<u>Pros:</u> Clubs can provide a way for teens to feel connected to a cause or express their values and beliefs to others.

Clubs can provide a way for teens to feel connected to a cause or express their values and beliefs to others.

Cons: Clubs say a lot about a person and can come back to haunt you on down the road when looking for a job. If you join "I cheated my way though college," don't be surprised if employers are not eager to hire you! Our teens need to be reminded (over and over again) that nothing they post is private. There is nothing wrong with expressing personal beliefs over heartfelt valid causes, but many of the clubs are senseless in nature and can speak volumes about a person's character.

Extra, Extra, Read All about It!

Facebook has become known as a primary means of staying up-to-date on the relationship status of your friends. Facebook gives the option of listing whether or not you are single, married, in a relationship, looking for friends, or "whatever I can get" (an actual option!). If you list that you are in a relationship, you are then given the option of submitting the person's name in your profile that hyperlinks to that person's Facebook profile page. A "newsfeed" that essentially gives a brief update of a sampling of actions taken by your friends often notifies users when a relationship status changes for someone on their friend list. For example, if two people who are previously listed as "in a relationship, break up and then change their status on Facebook to "single," it often notifies those on their friend lists of the change in the newsfeed. The newsfeed is the first page users see when they log onto their account. Look at it as a sort of daily newspaper highlighting the latest news concerning a person's online community of friends. It is similar to living in a small town and knowing everyone's business.

The town gossip in this case, is Facebook's news-feed feature, and it works around the clock, gathering up morsels of gossip. For example, a user may log on and read, "Tom Jones changed his profile picture," "Amanda Smith added '70s music to her list of favorite music," "Ryan Jenkins added new photos to his album, 'Young Life ski trip,'" "Will Gage and Brittany Sherman are no longer listed in a relationship," "Molly Culver joined the group 'I'm addicted to apple juice,'" "Katie Conner posted on Ian Shepherd's wall, 'hey loser, I heard you lost your new digital camera at the party,'" "Garrett Snyder commented on Chelsea Carter's picture, 'you look pretty wasted here,'" and the list goes on and on. Each update in the newsfeed comes complete with an exact time stamp of when the action took place and even thumbnail pictures of profile picture changes or a sampling from a newly added photo album.

Pros: The Facebook newsfeed can provide our students (and parents!) with tidbits of information about people on their friend list. Of course, this can be a good thing or a bad thing, depending on what that information is and how it is used. It can tip parents off to inappropriate pictures and comments, unhealthy friendships, upcoming parties, and the list goes on. It can only be accessed by logging on to your child's account but is guaranteed to provide a crash course on your child's peer group!

Cons: While your child has the option to block certain Facebook activities from being shared, they do not have complete control. Therefore, if they value their privacy (a foreign concept to most teens) and don't want to blast their entire friend list with updates on comments they've made to others, pictures they've uploaded, groups they've joined, information they've changed in their profile, or their relationship status, then they need to set the privacy options as high as possible and evaluate each and every move/keystroke. And they need to remember that grown-ups (such as myself) can log on and read the newsfeed.

What's a Parent to Do?

A June 2006 survey of 267 pairs of teens and parents in the Los Angeles metropolitan area by a psychology professor at California State University-Dominguez Hills found that two-thirds of parents had never talked with their teen about their MySpace use, and 38 percent of them had never seen their child's MySpace profile.[8] Findings such as this have spurred me on to write this book. This is not the malt shop, the skating rink, the mall, or the Sonic drive-thru. And trust me, this cyber hangout needs chaperones. While much media attention has been directed at the prevalence of predators on sites like MySpace, a new study conducted by a criminology professor at Florida Atlantic University and an assistant professor of criminal justice at the University of Wisconsin, Eau Claire, found that "most teens are behaving responsibly in the type of information they post about their lives."

The professors analyzed 1475 randomly selected profiles that appeared to be set up by teens and found that 90 percent of those allowing public viewing did not include the users' full names; 40 percent of the sample "were keeping their pages completely off-limits to everyone but their friends" (the default privacy setting for MySpace users who register as fourteen or fifteen years old); only 4 percent listed IM contact information; only 1 percent listed personal e-mail addresses; and "just a handful" listed their phone numbers. However, "more than half of teenagers posted their pictures online, and an unspecified number of others provided detailed physical descriptions of themselves." Additionally, 5 percent had pictures of themselves in swimsuits or underwear, and 15 percent of the profiles included suggestive pictures of their friends. (Yet another reason I cover the uploading of pictures and video in a separate chapter!). The researchers did find that even though 90 percent didn't list full names, "they left other identifying information, including their first names (40 percent), hometown (81 percent), and high school (28 percent)." In the end, the professors concluded that the benefits of social networking sites "far outweigh any potential risks."[9]

While I would never expect you to take the word of two professors you don't know, I agree that there is much good in the sites and that the key to a teen having a positive experience is parental involvement.

This brings me to the most common question I receive from parents: What is the appropriate age to participate in the sites? The answer will, of course, depend on the child in question. But let me say this:

if the child would have to lie about his age to meet the minimum age requirement, then no, obviously, that is not appropriate. I have been discouraged at the number of Christian kids I see participating in the sites who are underage. I realize their parents may not even know they have the profiles set up, but I wonder if some are just shrugging it off. Once your child meets the age requirement and you feel he is mature enough to handle the responsibility, I would require him to sign off on the safety contract I have provided in the appendix.

I also suggest that you require your children to give you their log-in information and password. I would emphasize that you are allowing them to have a page on a trial basis; and if you discover, after spot-checking their activity, that they have not proven themselves responsible, they will have to shut down their account.

Regardless of the child's age when he signs up for an account, I would be deeply involved on the front end. I would require that my child seek pre-approval on a profile picture and when changing to a new one. I would require that she not upload pictures to her page without your prior approval. I would require that she not list her last name, IM screen name, e-mail, or cell phone number. I would require that she set her page to private if she is on

MySpace and choose the privacy feature where no one can submit a friend request unless she knows their last name or e-mail address.

Facebook will list the school name and e-mail address. Facebook (at least at the time of this writing) is not accessible by those younger than high school age. It lists a minimum age of thirteen but rejects you unless you list the name of your high school. Younger kids not yet in high school are discouraged from lying and listing their future high school since they run the risk of being taunted by kids in the high school. High school students frown upon younger kids lying to get on Facebook, so many of the middle school kids set up profiles on MySpace instead. MySpace lists the minimum age as fourteen, but since no confirmation is required (at least at this time) to prove they are in high school, and it is easy to lie about their age before they turn fourteen, many turn to MySpace to set up a page.

Momma Has a MySpace Page

Yep, it's true. And for the record, I have a Facebook page too. Initially, I researched the sites by logging onto my daughter's account and surfing around to get a taste of what it was all about. It was clearly a teen's world. But then I began to notice something.

As stories began to circulate in the media about the dangers of the social networking sites, some adults responded by forbidding their children access to the sites while others moved onto the sites in droves to check it out for themselves. I decided to set up a profile in order to gain a true perspective of the social networking experience. And I must say, it has been an interesting experience. I set up my MySpace page as an author's page and rotated in various book covers as my profile picture. Within six weeks, I had more than two hundred friends, including some of my favorite Christian bands, other Christian speakers and authors, pastors, youth ministers, girls who have attended my events or read my books, women involved in girls' ministry, and concerned parents. I have quite an assortment of friends.

I was pleasantly surprised at the large number of Christian leaders who have a presence on MySpace, many in an attempt to reach this audience for Christ or maintain contact with the teens in their audience who were already on the sites. I have seen pages set up by teens that are a shining light for Christ in a place of darkness. Since I write to the audience of teens, I did not set my page to private in order that it could be yet another extension of my ministry outreach to teens. I use the blog feature to highlight articles in my *TeenVirtue* magabook series and address other issues affecting teens. Overall it has been a positive experience, and I have enjoyed hearing from others in the Christian community who are on my approved friend list. Occasionally I get a random friend request, and (upon checking out their page prior to accepting), I discover that they are not the type of person who would fall into my audience; therefore I decline the request (for example, an adult male from the UK who is obsessed with extra-terrestrials!). My presence on the site is a bit different from the average Christian parent who might set up a page. If I didn't have a public platform in ministry to teens and parents, I would set my page to private and be more selective about my friend list.

I have seen pages set up by teens that are a shining light for Christ in a place of darkness.

My Facebook page has been a much different story. All three of my children have Facebook pages, so I wanted to be careful not to appear that I was invading their space and showing up to police their activity. I decided that I would not send them a "friend request" but rather let them decide if they wanted

Mom on their list of friends. In the meantime, I had a few other adult friends to keep me company. We were able to post online albums and comment on one another's pictures, post messages to one another, and get a taste of what our teens enjoy about these sites.

Within a week of setting up my Facebook page, my two older children sent me a friend request. My third child did not have a page at the time but followed later. And a funny thing began to happen as the weeks and months progressed. I began to receive occasional friend requests from my kid's friends! In addition, my kids even sent friend requests to other parents they knew who had a Facebook profile and were on my friend list.

Much like MySpace, I use the page as an added outreach to my audience and a means to stay in contact with my own children. It has been especially enjoyable to keep up with my oldest son who is far away at college and take a peek at his pictures or send him a quick message of encouragement.

Overall, I have been impressed with my kids' pages, and I attribute it to the fact that my husband and I have been engaged in training our children to use technology in a responsible manner. They still make mistakes from time to time, and fortunately I have a presence on the sites (as well as direct access to my younger two children's accounts) to keep an eye on things and guide them along the way. While I can't guarantee that you will have the same results if you choose to set up a page, I encourage you to consider having a presence even if your children are not ready to send you a "friend request." You can always use the messaging feature to send them private messages of encouragement (even if they are not on your friend list). If you lay low and prove that you are not there to stalk their movements, you might be surprised to see a friend request from them in your in-box one day!

Keep the Conversation Going

As I have mentioned, I allow my children to participate on the sites but only because I monitor their pages on a consistent basis (with the exception of my college-age son). Before I would allow my children to participate, I had them sign off on a list of rules and expectations, or a contract, which I include in the appendix. And I continue to remind them of safety rules and take advantage of teachable moments as they arise. In other words, I did not engage them in a one-time online safety pep talk. It is an ongoing conversation in our home.

As I mentioned earlier, I have also required that my younger two children provide me with their log-in information and passwords to their Facebook and MySpace accounts. My daughter, who is seventeen, has proven herself more than trustworthy, and I no longer find it necessary to access her page by logging onto her account. I do, however, scan it on occasion by accessing it through my friend list just to ensure that she is not sharing too much information or allowing others to post information that could be misunderstood by others.

I know that much of what you have read thus far may be overwhelming, especially if you have never logged on to MySpace before reading this book. Even if you forbid your child from participating in the sites for the full eighteen years they live in your home (which I feel is extreme), you will not be able to shelter your child from the existence of the sites. I cannot imagine a child who has Internet access and never once logs onto one of the sites at a minimum to check out their friends' pages. My youngest child was not allowed to have a page until he met the minimum age requirement, but most of his friends set up profiles on MySpace by lying about their ages. You can wish it away all you want, but the reality is that by middle school you will have to address this issue because many of your child's friends will be on the sites. Their friends will hound them to get a MySpace page, and your child will want to check out their friends' pages.

Just as we try to shelter our children from other harmful messages they may receive through other media outlets, we can at least add a level of protection by drawing boundaries and teaching them the art of self-monitoring. Again, this does not mean we give them free reign to do as they please. I have been more than clear that I only endorse the use of social networking sites among our teens if there is parent involvement. The bottom line is that you can either be proactive or reactive when it comes to the social networking sites. You know your child best, so trust your gut when they begin to beg for a page. If they have one already, it's time to jump in, get your feet wet, and figure out what's going on. And if Momma (or Papa) gets a MySpace page, be sure to stop in and say "hi!"

CHAPTER 5

Pictures and Videos: Smile, You're on the World Wide Web!

Imagine that your son or daughter grows up and someday assumes the role of a public figure. Maybe he or she runs for public office or becomes a professional athlete or a much beloved teacher. Maybe they work for a Christian organization or receive a call to serve in ministry. And then imagine their dream is shattered when pictures emerge on the Web that compromise their reputation and question their character. Not likely, you say? Think again. With the prevalence of digital cameras and camera phones that can take unlimited pictures and shoot video clips, all it takes is one momentary lapse in good judgment. Just ask Miss Nevada 2007.

Whoops, I mean ex-Miss Nevada 2007. You might remember hearing about her in the news. She was stripped of her title after some interesting pictures cropped up on the Internet—pictures, I should note, that were taken five years prior to her receiving the state title. She was a mere seventeen years old at the time and learned the hard way that exposing your breasts, flashing your thong underwear, and kissing another girl are not acceptable behaviors for Miss USA state representatives. This story came on the heels of the reigning Miss USA's receiving a second chance from the Miss Universe organization after rumors emerged of excessive drinking, partying, and making out with Miss Teen USA. She was fortunate that pictures did not emerge to back up the rumors . . . at least not yet.

In an attempt to fight for her title and be given a second chance like Miss USA and Miss Teen USA, Miss Nevada had this to say in a press conference: "These photographs were from an isolated incident during my teenage years. This incident does not reflect who I am or whom I plan to be." She also offered this advice to young girls: "Please don't let your guard down when it comes to being photographed. As you can see, just one mistake can have a great consequence." Wise counsel from the crownless beauty queen. Our youth would be wise to learn from her mistake. One mistake can, years later, come back to haunt you in ways you never imagined.

While researching the top two social networking sites for this book, I came across picture after picture that could do serious damage to a reputation, career, or future dream in years to come. Let's see, there was a boy from my daughter's school whose profile picture is of him drinking bourbon straight from the bottle. A young lady posing in her black lacy bra. A picture of a girl at an outdoor concert holding a joint. Another girl at a concert taking hits from a bong. There were multitudes of pictures taken at weekend parties where alcohol was being consumed by the keg. One I saw even had a mother standing in the background laughing along with the teenagers. And for the record, I took a screen shot of that picture and saved it to my hard drive. Should any misfortune occur as a result of this woman's allowing minors to consume alcohol in her home, I would want to provide the police with evidence of her liability. I found that if the students are buzzing about an upcoming party (usually through Facebook, MySpace, and IMing), you can almost always guarantee that pictures will follow, sometimes just hours later, before their drunken haze has worn off.

Trust me when I say that students are ignorant to the fact that any parent, teacher, employer, college admissions office, or anyone for that matter who is not in their immediate circle of online friends would ever view their pictures. Just like Miss Nevada, many students probably never imagined that every time a flash goes off, their odds increase of showing up the following day in someone else's online picture albums—whether they want to be there or not. I can't tell you how many church kids I have stumbled across who have turned up in the background of pictures holding beer cans, smoking cigarettes, and engaged in other unwholesome acts, unaware that they were leaving a virtual bread-crumb trail of their actions.

Students are ignorant to the fact that any parent, teacher, employer, college admissions office, or anyone for that matter who is not in their immediate circle of online friends would ever view their pictures.

I should note that unless you have access to the social networking sites, it will be nearly impossible to monitor pictures taken of your child. Gone are the days of taking your film in to be developed. Our youth today store their pictures in albums online and rarely have them developed. Most of the pictures are uploaded directly to MySpace or Facebook in an online album feature. Even if you have access to the social networking sites, it will still be difficult to view photos taken by your child's friends since many profiles are set to private and only viewable by those on their friend list. Because of this, it is critical that parents educate their children to use good judgment when taking pictures, uploading pictures, having their pictures taken by others, and spot-checking their friends' albums to monitor the pictures they may be in. And remember, many of the pictures that an adult would deem to be inappropriate don't even make the radar when it comes to our youth.

It's Time to Talk

One theme I noticed while researching the top two social networking sites was the pattern of pictures being uploaded after holidays such as Halloween, Thanksgiving, Christmas, New Year's Eve, Valentine's Day, and spring break. Add to this homecoming, prom, graduation, and summer break; and you are guaranteed to see activity, especially among the girls. Momentous occasions call for digital cameras. Unlike our day of those hideous Kodak pocket cameras that took a whopping twelve to twenty-four photos, our children are equipped with digital cameras that have one gig memory cards and are capable of holding five hundred or more pictures. In addition, they are not required to take these photos to a lab to have them developed. A lab, mind you, that refuses to print photos containing nudity. This all translates into the ability to take literally hundreds of photos in one night with no rules of etiquette and no accountability. Given the increased traffic of picture uploading after holiday and school events, it might be a good idea to mark your calendar and broach the topic (again) of proper picture etiquette before the designated holiday or school activity. You also may want to check your children's online photo albums after the event to ensure they have abided by your rules.

Again, the goal is to teach our children to self-monitor, all the while offering them guidance along the way. Once they begin uploading pictures to the Web, it will be impossible for you to monitor every single photo they take or that is taken of them. You will not have the access needed to get into their friends' accounts, nor will you have the time to surf through each and every album that may contain a picture of your child. Therefore, parents must be diligent in offering their children's guidelines. The goal of this chapter is to equip you with observations, talking points, suggested rules, and even some real-life stories for the purpose of beginning conversations about this topic of pictures and videos. If only Miss Nevada had been so lucky as to have a parent go over this sort of information with her. Of course, in her situation, you would think that if she had a shred of common sense, it might have occurred to her that her unwholesome actions might produce unfortunate consequences.

This Trend Is Here to Stay

As digital cameras, camera phones, and the ability to take streaming video become a common mainstay among our teens, the trend toward user-generated content will become the norm in our culture. Let me explain what I mean by "user-generated content." In essence, technology has provided the average user (me, you, our children, etc.) the ability to generate content through blogs, video-sharing, and online picture albums to an audience of multimillions. Ordinary people now have the ability to be publishers, journalists, photographers, producers, and even stars of their own shows. There are no bounds to creativity, and no longer is it necessary to spend big bucks to reach an audience.

> **Ordinary people now have the ability to be publishers, journalists, photographers, producers, and even stars of their own shows.**

Take for example Gary Brolsma, a New Jersey teen who simply set up a Webcam in front of his computer monitor and filmed himself dancing to a catchy Romanian techno beat pop song. Think William Hung of *American Idol* here. Brolsma's now famous "Numa Numa Dance" video received over a million hits on one site alone within months of its release. If you have a child in your home who is fifteen or older, they probably saw it. No producer. No multimillion-dollar marketing campaign. Just traditional grassroots word-of-mouth and, voila, the kid was famous overnight. What we are witnessing today is a shift from mass communications-driven media to people-generated media. The power is truly with the people.

Take for example YouTube (youtube.com), a popular site where videos can be uploaded and accessed by the public. It had close to 900,000 viewers in November 2005. A year later it had increased to 25.5 million visitors in the month of November. Apparently, Google was impressed with the 2,720 percent change in increased traffic and bought the homegrown video site for $1.7 billion.[1] On YouTube you will find video clips of everything imaginable, including sermon clips from your favorite Christian ministers, music videos, graduation speeches, highlights from football games, bloopers, and homemade videos of every kind. In the process of writing this book, my son sent me an e-mail with a link to a video he and some of his college buddies posted to YouTube. They were imitating an old Back Street Boys' hit song in the corridors of their dorm. It was precious, and within weeks the clip had received more than three thousand views.

Unfortunately you will also find countless inappropriate clips that range from bad language, pornography, cruelty to animals, embarrassing pranks, and illegally downloaded TV shows and music videos.

YouTube has provided an easy-to-use format to expose videos almost real-time to tens of millions of people. It has highlighted videos of screaming teachers in the classroom (taken from a student's cell phone), fights on school buses and in back alleys, cops tasering suspects, and celebrities behaving badly. You might remember the story that hit the news concerning the racial tirade of comedian Michael Richards *(Seinfeld)* during a comedy routine. The whole thing was filmed by someone in the audience and uploaded to YouTube the following day.

A day after Britney Spears broke up with Kevin Federline by text message, you could view a video clip of Kevin receiving the actual text message while sitting at a table in a restaurant. Another clip of Tom Cruise surfaced as he was followed by paparazzi on his way to the men's room at one of his son's soccer games. It was noteworthy because it showed a toddler being knocked down by the paparazzi as they attempted to catch up with Tom. The baffled mother was caught on camera screaming at Tom Cruise for just standing there and staring at the crying child on the ground after it happened. Clearly anything is fair game on YouTube. With the prevalence of video cameras, not to mention cameras and cell phones that have the capability of filming short video clips, we will see more and more homemade clips showing up on the Web.

Rather than throw the baby out with the bathwater and declaring this whole forum evil, we again need to teach our children to self-monitor when it comes to uploading pictures and video to the Web.

It is hard to ban video sites like YouTube since clips are often sent as links through e-mail, IM, and the social networking sites. MySpace provides within the template of their standard profile page a place for video uploads, and it is not uncommon to find several video-clip favorites loaded straight to someone's page. They are virtually unavoidable. It might be perfectly fine for your twelve-year-old to click on a link sent in an e-mail from a friend advertising streaming video of a cat jumping from a tree, but once a video ends up on the YouTube site, they may be exposed to other video clips that aren't as innocent. Many Internet filters on the market today allow parents to block certain sites or have the ability to tag inappropriate sites and block access. I highly recommend installing one of these filters.[2] It is not 100 percent foolproof, but it adds another level of protection. Most importantly, parents must be aware of the dangers associated with uploading pictures and video and must be diligent in passing along safety tips to their children.

It is hard to ban video sites like YouTube since clips are often sent as links through e-mail, IM, and the social networking sites.

Our kids need to know that pictures and videos taken in the present or past can ruin your reputation years later. For Miss Nevada the pictures are here to stay, forever and ever. Actually, they will be around long after she breathes her last breath. Certainly a humbling thought when you think that her children, grandchildren, and future generations will have access to her unfortunate antics at a party when she was a mere teen. Not something I would want to find out about my mother or grandmother! This is also a good time to remind your child that even pictures and videos once removed are most likely still alive and well on a hard drive somewhere. If your child ever becomes known someday, rest assured, any video or photo from years before is likely to reappear. Someone somewhere will remember and bring old images into the present, particularly if those images can do damage.

Most of the damaging pictures I have found are linked to alcohol. Because most of our youth have digital cameras and camera phones, they have instant access at every party to life's most embarrassing moments. If a girl has too much to drink and decides to flash her breasts or accept a dare to kiss another girl, why wouldn't someone snap a picture of that or make a streaming video of it on their phone? Of course it will show up on the Web, and your children need to know that. And the more you drink, the greater the odds that you will do some really stupid things that can follow you for years to come. I have witnessed pictures on Facebook of students throwing up, urinating, making out, flashing their private parts, and other drunken misdeeds.

Because most of our youth have digital cameras and camera phones, they have instant access at every party to life's most embarrassing moments.

Girls who flash their breasts and make out with other girls may be told they are "hot" by the guys, but in reality they are labeled sluts by most of the public. Pictures of this nature indicate an extremely low self-esteem and signal much deeper problems. Again, as Miss Nevada discovered, many drew conclusions about her moral character (or lack thereof) based on pictures taken years ago at one party. Her reputation was sealed, and the damage is done. Since the Miss Universe organization touts the moral character of their contestants (oh, puhleese!), they concluded that she was not a match for the title she had been given.

I want to share some observations I made while in the process of researching for this book that will help parents better understand the reality of what they will find when they surf through the online photo album of the average high schooler. These observations are worthy of mention because they merit a few additional talking points that must be addressed by parents. Most are directed at parents of daughters, and this shouldn't come as a surprise, given they are more likely to own a digital camera, take multitudes of pictures, and upload the pictures to countless online albums. Whether you have a daughter or not, it would be beneficial for you to be aware of the climate.

Observation 1. Apparently, it is now a compliment for a girl to be called a whore or slut by her friends. I cannot tell you how many times I stumbled across a picture of a girl posing seductively with a come-hither expression on her face only to find that other girls (her friends, presumably) had left comments beneath the picture to the effect of, "Hannah, you look like such a whore in this picture! I love it!" Or how about, "What a little slut you are! I am so jealous!" Since when did it become in vogue to look like a whore?

Observation 2. What's up with the Halloween costumes girls are wearing? I have never seen so many pictures of sexy nurses, scantily clad cow-girls, Playboy bunnies, French maids, racy referees, and sultry Indian princesses. And mind you, many of these girls were church girls. The skirts were so short you could sometimes see the bottom part of their buttocks. There was plenty of exposed cleavage, fishnet stockings, and stilettos to top it off. It also appears to be the fashion to unbutton blouses to expose your lacy Victoria's Secret bras. My daughter didn't participate in any of the parties in question, but plenty of girls from her school did. And the problem appears not to be an isolated event just at her school. I witnessed girls from all over the city representing a variety of different high schools dressed in this fashion. It looked like a porn convention of sorts. Is it any wonder women are treated more like objects today than ever before? Enough is enough. Please keep this in mind if you have daughters. Even if you think your daughter would never dress this way, know that many of her friends will. Girls will often leave the house dressed one way and change at a friend's house, especially if they are accustomed to getting grief at home about their wardrobe. Again, if you are checking your daughter's pictures, you will know if she is partici-pating in this new form of dress-up.

Observation 3. There's a lot of skin out there. Many girls think nothing of posting pictures from a pool party or a day spent at the lake. To them it's just a day of fun, and they are blind to the fact that predators love nothing more than to find pictures of minor-aged girls in swimwear, low-cut blouses, short shorts, and tight T-shirts exposing bare midriffs. A friend of mine recently shared a story about running into a dad at a coffee shop. His daughter and my friend's daughter run in the same group of girls. She asked how his daughter was doing; and he beamed with pride as he went on and on about her volunteer work at a shelter, straight-A report cards, and her solid value system. He ended by saying, "She has a good head on her shoulders, and we couldn't be more proud of her." What he didn't know was that his daughter has some of the most provocative pictures you can imagine posted on the Web. Pictures of her in a string bikini top exposing her cleavage for the camera. Pictures of her lying out on a towel in the same string bikini. Picture after picture of her posing seductively and sending a clear message that "if you've got it, flaunt it." Unfortunately, it didn't line up with the same message her dad had passed along to my friend!

Many girls think nothing of posting pictures from a pool party or a day spent at the lake.

Observation 4. Girls like to kiss each other on the cheek. In the cases I witnessed (and there were many), it appeared innocent and sisterly. I'm not here to judge whether or not it is right or wrong and will leave that one for you to decide. I only mention it because it may catch you off guard if you begin surfing through some of these online albums. At the very least, we need to sit our daughter down and address the inappropriateness of kissing girls on the mouth, even if it is meant as a joke and for the sake of a picture.

Observation 5. Forget the Boone's Farm Tickled Pink and Country Quencher. Kids today are into hard liquor and a lot of it. I couldn't help but notice the multitude of pictures of high school students taking tequila shots, mixing drinks, drinking from beer bongs, and holding vodka bottles. Mind you, these were high school students. As someone who didn't come to Christ until late college, I did my fair share of drinking in late high school and college. Even when I was attending the University of Texas and was invited to attend numerous frat parties, never did I witness the prevalence of hard liquor as I have in these photos. I can only imagine the devastating fallout this will produce in the years to come.

Observation 6. There are a lot of clueless, uncaring, irresponsible parents out there. While doing my research for this chapter, over and over again I would shake my head back and forth and ask, "Where in the world are the parents?" My goal was not to play good cop/bad cop by tattling to parents about immoral actions I had witnessed in pictures. However, I did discuss some of my findings along the way with other parents. I found that the parents usually fell into one of two camps when I discussed many of the observations I listed above.

One camp of parents seemed clueless as to the depth of the problem but showed valid concern. Their ignorance was only because they were unaware of the dangers associated with their child's wired world and not sure how to catch up. Hopefully, they will find this book to be a helpful resource.

The other camp of parents was clueless and shrugged off the situation as no big deal. The "aw, kids will be kids" response. Of course, this is the camp of parents that makes me want to bang my head up against a concrete wall . . . or better yet, their heads. And typically, as a rule, their kids have some of the most incriminating pictures on the Web. The truth is, there are parents out there who are absent for all practical purposes. Their children have no boundaries, no rules; and they have digital cameras and free rein to do as they please online and offline. Unfortunately, the parents of such kids are not likely to be reading this book.

A Picture Is Worth a Thousand Words

In addition to going over the safety rules related to the uploading of pictures and videos that I have provided in the appendix, parents should also be on guard for the latest stories in the news or on the rumor mill that deal with fallout from pictures and videos being posted to the Web. The goal is to use them as teachable moments with our children in order to help them learn from others' mistakes. Below, you will find a few real-life stories that I have taken the liberty to share with my children for the purpose of reminding them of the *why* behind the rules above.

1. Talented singer: *American Idol* contestant Antonella Barba had rather compromising pictures surface on the Internet. When interviewed by *People* magazine and asked about the pictures, she said: "Yes, it's true that my name is more well-known

because of it, but I'm not known for the things that I would like to be known for right now. I wanted to make a name for myself in singing. The pictures that have been released of me—the ones that actually are me—they were very personal and that is not how I intended to portray myself. I'd rather promote myself in a more classy way."

2. High school teacher from Austin, Texas: A recent scandal in my city involved a high school teacher who was found to have a MySpace profile that contained pictures of her drinking and posing topless. She lost her job over the matter due to an outcry among the parents. Unfortunately, the pictures were discovered by her students, and word spread like wildfire.

3. Cheerleaders behaving badly: A story recently emerged in the news about pictures posted online of a group of cheerleaders in a suburb of Dallas who posed brazenly, making suggestive gestures in front of a condom store. The scandal rocked the community.

My daughter is a varsity cheerleader, and her coach recently announced that she had access to their Facebook and MySpace profiles and pictures (through a student intern, I presume) and was disturbed over some of the pictures she discovered. Among other unwholesome behaviors, she specifically mentioned girls holding beer cans at parties. She reminded them of their responsibility to be positive role models and leaders both on and off campus. Our children need to know that many coaches and school officials are checking the social networking sites on a regular basis.

> **Our children need to know that many coaches and school officials are checking the social networking sites on a regular basis.**

4. News account of Republican nominee for a Senate seat race in Tennessee and an untimely picture captured of his daughter on Facebook: The candidate was running on a conservative family values platform, and the opposing side unearthed a picture on Facebook of his college-age daughter making out with another girl at a party. I'm sure the picture has since been removed from Facebook, but it has found a second life on other sites on the World Wide Web. One blog page for the other side had this to say, "You'd think Mr. ****** might have let his lovely daughter know that she probably shouldn't let

pictures of her making out with chicks and dancing at underwear parties show up on a publicly accessible social networking Web site. Thankfully for all of you, they never had that talk."

As an interesting side note to the story, a comment was posted on the blog story by one of her friends who came to her defense and said this: "Her friend (who took the picture) just posted a harmless drunken picture on Facebook, and everyone's freaking out over nothing." Did you catch that, parents? "Her friend" posted the picture. And to the young lady that posted the comment above, I would argue that it was anything but harmless. If you google the name of this candidate's daughter, you will find page after page listing links to the picture of this "harmless" kiss. I'm betting she's a bit more aware now when others snap her picture at a party. (Note: I have chosen not to post the name of this family out of respect for their privacy . . . or what's left of it at this point.)

5. Pastor's daughter dressed inappropriately: I was recently tipped off to a blog page that was discussing a pastor of a large megachurch and a controversy surrounding some issues that were causing division in the church. Unrelated to the controversy, someone posted a comment stating that there was a picture on Facebook of the pastor's high school-age

daughter wearing a rather revealing top. I think it is completely inappropriate and below the belt to drag someone's minor-age daughter through the mud in an attempt to make the point that a pastor who can't lead his family can't lead a church. However, I bring it up as a humbling reminder that those of us in leadership are held to higher standards. Given the current technological advancements, it is now possible to put someone's spouse and children under the microscope with a few clicks of a mouse.

One Final Thought

Finally, let me encourage you to do one more thing before you begin to address this topic with your child. Remember back to when you were in middle school, high school, and college. Think back on the parties you attended: homecoming, prom, graduation, and even the average weekend spent perhaps at the local teen hangout. Now imagine that you have a digital camera that can fit in your pocket and is capable of taking hundreds of pictures. Maybe you aren't the picture-taking type; therefore imagine that others in your peer group are. Imagine that you and your friends can upload unlimited photos straight to the Web. What sort of pictures might show up based on your behavior in those years?

This is a humbling thought for many of us. I immediately flashed back to a time when my friends and I took pictures of one another in our dorm rooms at cheerleading camp, posing for the camera in our bras and underwear. Amazingly, the pictures were developed. What in the world were we thinking? I wonder if one of us might have been stupid enough to upload them to the Web if the technology had existed? I'm betting so, and I wouldn't be surprised if I was the one to do it!

I think back on other events I attended that were fortunately not documented in pictures. Because developing pictures was expensive, we were deterred from carrying a camera around with us at all times. And thank goodness for that. I can't even begin to imagine what might be circulating somewhere on the Web had today's technology been present when I was a teen.

What about you? Reflect on that thought before you address the dangers with your own children, and do your best to give them the benefit of the doubt. They are more likely to receive your counsel if you approach the situation with humility and a sincere concern to protect them from harm. As I reflect on the mistakes I made in my teen years, I for one am extremely grateful that digital cameras and the Internet were not a part of those years.

CHAPTER 6

Caution—Danger Ahead! Avoiding the Pitfalls of a Digital World

As we come to a close, I want to commend you for staying with me this far. I know much of what you have read has been overwhelming at times. Kudos to you for not giving up. I want to take an opportunity in this final chapter to leave you with a summation of the primary dangers our children are currently facing in this new and burgeoning digital world. In addition, I have also included additional talking points and safety contracts pertaining to IMing, cell phones, social networking sites, and picture/video uploading in the appendix. In addition, they can be downloaded on www.loggedonandtunedout.com. Hopefully you have been highlighting as you have read the preceding chapters and will take some time to discuss what you have learned with your child(ren).

Online Overtime

More and more often we are hearing about online addictions. If you have a child over fourteen, you have probably experienced the parent-child battle over too much time spent online. There are no hard-and-fast rules that tell us what exactly constitutes "too much," so most parents are left to come up with their own reasonable guidelines when it comes to computer use. Since this generation is marked by the fact that they multitask and move back and forth between different modes of technology, it is hard to determine whether or not their time spent online is in balance. Are they doing homework? Are they IMing friends? Are they checking their MySpace/Facebook page? Are they doing all three at the same time? Chances are good that they are.

As parents, we cannot watch over their shoulders every minute of every day, but we can implement monitoring software to do it for us. Check your detailed reports to see how many minutes your child is spending on sites such as MySpace, Facebook, YouTube, gaming sites, and other sites that may be of interest to them. Pay attention to how much time is spent IMing their friends on an average day. You should be able to discern in the reports which sites are related to homework and which are related to leisure.

Also, be on the lookout for signs that your child has become too dependent on the computer. Is it hard for them to pull away when you call them to the dinner table? Are their grades falling? Do they rush to the computer immediately when they get home? Are they snappy and irritable with you or others in your home who try to talk to them while they are online? Consider having this rule: no computer until homework is done. If they have homework assignments where the computer is needed, consider telling them they cannot engage in online leisure activities until they are done.

Also consider having a computer curfew if you notice your child is using it late into the night. When my oldest son was spending too much time playing online games in his senior year of high school, I activated a control on our safety filter that shuts the computer off at a designated time of my choosing. Since he was old enough to be on the computer after my husband and I went to bed, I programmed it to shut off at midnight. The first night it happened (I warned him in advance!), I heard a blood-curdling scream when it threw him off the Internet at the stroke of midnight. Unfortunately, it happened right in the middle of an online game. It was a tough lesson for him, but after awhile he began to pay attention to the clock and wrap up his game before the computer wrapped it up for him. It was, no doubt, a critical lesson he needed to learn before heading out the door for college the following year.

Michael Bugeja, director of Iowa State University's journalism school and author of the book *Interpersonal Divide: The Search for Community in a Technological Age,* said, "Each year, incoming students are more distracted than ever."[1] If we don't teach our children the art of self-restraint, especially in regard to their logged-on lives, they may not survive the first semester away from home.

Psychologists and Internet experts say they are seeing a growing number of kids who are addicted to being online. These same experts say that kids who are socially insecure tend to be more vulnerable than others. If they are heavily dependent on what others think, it should come as no surprise that they would prefer to spend time in an environment where they have multitudes of virtual online friends. Many of these students will spend hours a day sending texts and posting comments to their friends in a desperate attempt to keep the communication going. Every time they log on to an in-box full of messages or wall posts and receive a coveted friend request, they feel the same type of momentary thrill that an alcoholic may feel when taking a drink. If you feel that your child is susceptible to an online addiction, limit the time spent online and help your teen build face-to-face relationships.

Identity Crisis

There has been much debate over whether the profiles teens create on the social networking sites are a reflection of their true selves at that time or rather an ideal of what they wish they were. No doubt, it is easy to hide behind a computer monitor and pretend to be someone you're not. While some teens lie when filling out their profile information (even subconsciously), most seem to lay it all out there with a sort of attitude that says, "What you see is what you get." Whether the pictures and/or text depict a true representation of the person is up for debate. I recently saw someone wearing a shirt bearing the logo, "You looked better on MySpace." Clearly, what you see is not always what you get!

When setting up profiles, users can either present their authentic self or the persons they wish they were. Whether the end result is more fact or fiction, it boils down to a description of the person they desperately want others to see.

Danah Boyd, a pioneering social-networks researcher at the University of California, Berkeley, says, "Although it may look aimless and superficial, it's actually very productive." She also says that a site like MySpace is "not the waste of time adults think it is," and goes on to state that "informal learning" is taking place when teens spend time putting together their profiles and describing who they are as a person and listing their associated likes and dislikes.[2]

David Huffaker, a researcher of online social behavior at Northwestern University, makes the argument that social networking sites can have a positive impact on identity development for teens. "These activities are important for identity exploration, which is one of the principal tasks of adolescence."[3]

While I agree to some degree with the opinions stated above and think that it can be a positive exercise, especially for Christian teens who desire to stand as a light for Christ and boldly let the world know who they are, I also caution parents that it can be disastrous for teens who are insecure and struggling to find their place in the world. Teens are known for going through awkward phases in their quest for self-discovery. How many of us know an adult who has managed to make a marvelous transition from a one-time rebellious teen to an upstanding moral citizen today? If MySpace had been around in the 1960s and 1970s, how many hippies would we find in the archives with embarrassing photos displayed from their days of Woodstock? I for one am glad that MySpace was not around in my teen years!

As parents, we need to point out to our teens that the person they present themselves to be on the sites today may come back to haunt them tomorrow. While our generation has the luxury of looking back at our teen years and shrugging it off with a casual, "What was that all about?" our teens today are not so fortunate. Unbeknownst to them, they are documenting their journey of self-discovery for all to see. It's up to us to remind them of this fact often.

As parents, we need to point out to our teens that the person they present themselves to be on the sites today may come back to haunt them tomorrow.

Offline Communication

A 2005 report for Achieve, a nonprofit organization that helps states raise academic standards, found that 34 percent of employers were dissatisfied with the oral communication skills of high school graduates and that 45 percent of college students and 46 percent of high school graduates who entered the workforce instead of college said they struggled with their public speaking abilities.[4]

Will the shift in the way our teens communicate via their phones and keyboards come with a price? Many say it will. Sonya Hamlin, author of *How to Talk So People Listen: Connecting in Today's Workplace*, says, "We are losing very natural, human, instinctive skills that we used to be really good at." A couple of years ago, she was asked to teach a class of "very bright" California high school seniors about the college admissions interview. Their mock answers were "extremely short and not informational. Nothing came out, really, because it's such an unused skill." Heather Hogan, a Nassau Community College freshman from Bellmore, New York, said, "No one talks, really, unless you're with people."[5]

The counterargument to this is that instant messaging, texting, cell phones, and social networking sites have afforded our teens the ability to stay in touch and exchange more messages with more friends than would otherwise be possible if they were simply limited to face-to-face contact. The key, as is often the case, is balance. It will be up to parents to pull the plug or take up the phone if they see that face-to-face communication is limited and social skills are lacking. I can't help but wonder if the lack of interpersonal communication skills is not linked more to the decrease in the amount of quality family time. If you make it a habit to sit around the dinner table and require your children to answer your questions in more than just standard monosyllables of *yes* and *no*, that table talk will go a long way in the effort to build your children's face-to-face communication skills.

It will be up to parents to pull the plug or take up the phone if they see that face-to-face communication is limited and social skills are lacking.

Cyberbullying

As someone who has written on the subject of girl politics and mean girls, I have a news flash:

With the popularity of MySpace and Facebook, girl politics just got meaner. And to make matters worse, the boys have now joined the club. The fact that teens will typically type things they would never say to someone's face makes the Internet the new breeding ground for a dangerous strain of cyber-hate, a strain that can produce devastating fallout for years to come. Friendships have ended over not being included in another friend's "top eight friend list" on MySpace. Feelings have been hurt over discovering pictures on Facebook of the boy you like with his arm around another girl. But the stressors above hardly make the radar when compared to the wave of cyberbullying that is commonplace on the social networking sites. A recent study found that one in three twelve- to seventeen-year-olds have been victims of cyberbullying. In an Internet survey of about fourteen hundred young people, 34 percent of the respondents reported having been bullied online. About 40 percent of the teens surveyed said they had been "disrespected"; 13 percent said they felt threatened by their online exchange; and 5 percent said they feared for their safety.[6]

"Kids are natives to the Internet, and adults are the immigrants," says Elizabeth Englander of the Massachusetts Aggression Reduction Center. "Adults, being so far behind the eight ball, means we won't be able to educate kids on cyberbullying." Englander says it creates a "perfect storm" in which kids have a separate, unmonitored universe where they can be naive enough to think there are no consequences. Stories are emerging in the news of everything from students posting lists of the sluttiest girls in the school to girls taking their camera phones into the locker room and getting back at girls they don't like by posting their pictures on the Web.[7]

The Internet also allows kids to impersonate one another, something that's nearly impossible to do in a school hallway. Last year five schoolmates at a St. Louis high school decided to post a "hot/not hot" list of more than one hundred female classmates, with racist and sexist comments, on Facebook. They signed the name of a seventeen-year-old junior, who learned of the list only when one of the girls asked him about it. "He was mortified," says Nancy, the boy's mother, who asked to use her first name only. "It was incredibly upsetting, and we were absolutely powerless."[8]

Researcher David Nelson says the Internet can play on teens' weaknesses. "This cyberbullying stuff, especially the instant, spontaneous nature of it, really plays on vulnerabilities of adolescence, because they have an underdeveloped sense of empathy in terms of how their actions affect others," Nelson says. "If somebody fires a zinger at you, it's very easy to then get upset and immediately respond to it with a zinger of your own."[9] And if someone breaks up with your best friend, it's easy to retaliate via the Internet—or so I discovered recently while spot-checking my own daughter's Facebook activity. While she has been spared thus far from this new strain of cyberhate, some of her friends have not. One girl at her high school is in the process of transferring to a different school in an attempt to pick up the pieces of her tattered reputation, ruined in the matter of a few minutes with a few clicks of a mouse.

To give you a better idea of the seriousness of cyberbullying, let me give you a brief time line of what happened to the girl in the incident above. When logging onto my daughter's Facebook account to spot-check her activity (something I do every couple of weeks), I noticed that she had received an invitation to join a Facebook group that a guy at her high school had created. The name of the group was controversial in nature, so I clicked through to read the description. What I found left me absolutely speechless. This guy had created a group for the sheer purpose of listing another girl's alleged sex partners. From what I could gather, he apparently created the group in an attempt to retaliate after the girl broke up with his best friend. The fake sex list even included a picture of the high school principal, lifted straight from the school's Web site. What was particularly disturbing was the fact that this guy set up the group in the girl's name, using her profile picture, lifted straight from her Facebook page, and described the alleged sexual accounts in first person as if she were the author. He then sent an "invite" out to his friends (also fellow students) to join the group, and within a twenty-four-hour period, more than one hundred students from the high school had joined the group. As if it couldn't get much worse, some of the students who joined the group then posted their thoughts about this young lady and the rumors surrounding the breakup. Some of the most vicious comments posted came from girls, many of whom had at one point or another been in this girl's peer group.

Fortunately, in the situation above, the girl's parents were eventually notified by a concerned parent (cough, cough). The young man who had set up the page was suspended from school for several days and received a gentle slap on the wrist. The girl's father submitted a complaint to Facebook who in turn deleted the group and his Facebook account within hours of receiving the complaint. However, within days, his account was back up and running. He did not attempt to restore the group but was able to rebuild his profile page. While this young lady was fortunate enough to have her parents step in before it could escalate any further, it is far from a happy ending. Even though the group has been deleted, the impact will remain forever etched in her mind.

Few students realize that the results could have been fatal as stories are beginning to emerge in the media of students killing themselves over being the target of cyberbullying incidents. Discuss the dangers of cyberbullying with your children. It is easy to get swept up into the wrong crowd with a few clicks of a mouse. The familiar cliché, "Do unto others as you would have them do unto you," is a great motto to go over with our kids when it comes to their behavior, both offline and online. They will have many opportunities to take part in various forms of cyberbullying whether they are the instigator or part of the lynch mob. Encourage your kids to decide up front that they will not take part in activities that would cause harm to others. Also, have them be on the lookout for others who are being victimized by online bullies. If the offense is serious, they should contact a trusted adult and ask him or her to get involved before it escalates any further. Who knows—their efforts just might save a life.

The familiar cliché, "Do unto others as you would have them do unto you," is a great motto to go over with our kids when it comes to their behavior, both offline and online.

Finally, if parents are to combat the problem of cyberbullying, they must be willing to monitor what their kids are doing and saying online. Had the parents of the girl above been monitoring her activity, they would have been aware of the situation much earlier in the game. Most importantly, parents must make it clear to their children that cyberbullying will not be tolerated. Social networking sites, instant messaging, and text messaging will present them with many opportunities to be the cyberbully or a part of a cyberbully gang, so parents need to draw a firm boundary before the temptation presents itself. Should they cross the line, consider forbidding them from all means of "instant communication" until they prove they are mature enough to handle the responsibility.

Porn

If children are looking for porn, they can find it on every forum of communication we have discussed in this book. Even if parents ban their children completely from accessing the Internet and owning a cell phone (good luck!), it is only a matter of time before they will stumble upon porn. I elaborated on this topic in my book *Your Boy: Raising a Godly Son in an Ungodly World* and presented the need to train our sons (and daughters) to self-monitor. This is, of course, in addition to setting appropriate boundaries such as installing an Internet safety filter and monitoring software.[10]

Our children must learn to "bounce their eyes" (a concept introduced in Steve Arterburn's book *Every Young Man's Battle*) in an attempt to shield themselves from the constant barrage of inappropriate images. In addition, parents must be diligent in explaining why it is damaging to view porn. Our boys especially must be told that viewing porn will give them an unrealistic view of sex and can produce damaging consequences on down the road in marriage. Further, they need to be told that it degrades women by painting them as nothing more than objects for the viewing pleasure of men. The world is telling them that it is acceptable and a natural part of growing up. We must speak up and dispel the lies of the culture.

The sad truth is, we will not be able to completely shield our children from inappropriate images in today's culture, so we must prepare them with a battle plan. Just as when our boys are walking through the local mall and pass by a lingerie storefront, they are faced with a choice. Will they avert their eyes and move on, or will they stop and stare? Or even worse, will they venture into the store to further satisfy their curiosity? The same is true with technology. They will be presented with inappropriate "storefronts" from time to time, and the goal is to keep them moving, all the while averting their eyes.

The sad truth is, we will not be able to completely shield our children from inappropriate images in today's culture, so we must prepare them with a battle plan.

Predators

I'm sure by now you've probably heard a fair share of disturbing stories regarding predators who troll sites like MySpace looking for vulner-able kids. Overall, the media attention brought a much-needed awareness to parents about the dangers involved in allowing their children unlimited access to the social networking sites. MySpace has since made strides in tightening security on the site; and while it is not 100 percent safe, it is much improved.

You might remember a study that I referred to in chapter 4 that found that "most teens are behaving responsibly in the type of information they post about their lives." Another study by California State University-Dominguez Hills pro-fessor Larry Rosen featured interviews with more than fifteen hundred MySpace.com users, and in his research he found that only 7 percent of teen MySpace.com users he interviewed reported hav-ing been approached by anyone with a sexual intent. Rosen further said, "When you look at what kind of things are happening, where they're being solicited, it has nothing to do with preda-tors. It has to do a lot with friends, with other people saying, 'Hey, you want to get it on?' But they're not predators—they're usually people their age.'"[11] And based on my research, I would have to agree. Even in the midst of a media campaign where I did more than one hundred interviews on

Internet safety that focused primarily on the issue of Internet predators, I kept wondering when the media would catch on to the even bigger problem on these sites: the teens themselves and the lack of parent supervision!

In the process of researching for a book I recently wrote to teen girls, I surveyed a sampling of girls (most are church girls) and asked them the following question: "Have you ever been contacted by a stranger online and made to feel uncomfortable? If yes, explain what happened and whether or not you told your parents."

Below, you will find a sampling of their answers. I share them with you for the purpose of encouraging you to be engaged in what your teens are doing online. If you choose not to be engaged, your daughter could have a story like one of the ones below.

_____

Yes, I have, especially on MySpace. I get messages and friend invites all the time and things that say like you're hot and stuff. I usually look at their page and see if I know them, and if I don't then I send them a message asking how they know me. If I have no clue who they are and they are just a random person, then I avoid them and end all contact with that person. And no, I don't usually tell my parents about it. —Ashley, 14

I have people contact me online all the time through MySpace or IM. If they don't leave me alone, sometimes I tell my parents. —Donna, 15

I was on AIM and this random guy is like 'hey' and I'm like 'um do I know you?' and he said, 'nope,' so I looked at his profile. It had a link to porn, so I blocked him. —Kinsey, 15

One time on MySpace a grown man asked me to be his 'friend' (it's a MySpace thing) and I replied with a no. I didn't tell my parents, but I told my friends and they said that has happened to them before too. —Madeline, 12

Yes I was online talking to my friends, and this guy started talking to me and I had no idea who he was. When I asked him who he was, he told me that I should remember because we had had cybersex. . . . I had never even talked to this person before. —Amanda, 15

This person started IMing me on AOL instant messenger, I was about twelve or thirteen, and I was too naive to know the difference, so I kept talking with him. After a few weeks he started freaking me out, saying he loved me and all that jazz. . . . I blocked him real quick! Thankfully, I never gave him any of my personal info or anything. I never told my parents about it. —Amanda, 17

Yes, I have. I was in a Christian chat room. I guess this guy was watching me for some time. He said he was a Christian. He gained my trust. He had a Webcam and asked me if I wanted to see his face. I said 'sure.' I saw his face and then he brought it down to his private parts. —Aspen, 17

Yes, I have. It was really weird and he asked me inappropriate questions and I was very uncomfortable. I blocked him and logged off. I never told my parents. —Jordan, 13

Yes, he sent me a message on MySpace saying that I looked 'totally hott!' and he wanted to meet me sometime because we lived in the same town. I just blocked him and completely ignored the message. I didn't tell my parents because I was afraid they would want me to get off MySpace because of it. —Louisa, 14

I was playing a game on miniclip where you had a chance to talk. I normally didn't but one time a guy wanted to know if I wanted to . . . do something that was wrong. I told my parents, and now if anyone talks to me during an online game, I forfeit. —Lynlee, 14

Well I used to have a Xanga site open to the public. This guy started sending messages like 'I would love to put you on the cam babe' or

*'we should hook up' and other wrong things.
I showed my mom the least embarrassing
things, and she said I needed to delete my site.
At the time I was bummed. I thought I could
just block that person. But now after looking
back I know she was right. —Crystal, 14*

---

*Yes one time I had a guy start talking to me
online. He supposedly lived in my area and
went to my school. At first I thought nothing
of it until he started trying to get really personal. I told my dad and it ended up that this
guy lived about a state away and he was in his
early thirties. —Chrystal, 16*

---

*Yes there was this guy that found me through
MySpace before there was the privacy option
where you could block people you didn't know.
I never told him anything about me because
I had heard so many stories about young girls
getting involved with someone from the Internet
and getting raped, and sometimes killed.
I chose not to tell my mom because I was
too afraid of her shutting down my MySpace,*

*and I didn't think I was in danger or at least
I thought. Then I got a text message one day
from him! I guess in a comment from a friend
they asked me if I still had the same cell number then they listed it and that's how he got it.
He was nineteen years old and this was starting to freak me out, but I never replied to his
messages. Then he tried calling me and I never
answered. Finally, he gave up. That was last
summer, but sometimes I wonder what would
have happened if I replied. Now, my profile is
set to private, and I never talk to anyone I don't
know. —Amanda, 15*

---

*Yes, there have been numerous times when
boys or men will ask me where I live. Of course
I don't tell them and I try to ignore them. No,
I didn't tell my parents. —Teresa, 17*

---

*Yes. I was on MySpace and he commented on
my pictures in my profile. . . . I didn't tell my
parents because I was ashamed that I mes-
saged him back. —Jennifer, 14*

*Yes, and we talked for like a year and then we
broke up. No, I didn't tell my parents.*
—Alisia, 14

While the information from the survey above
is sobering, I want to point out that the common
denominator in the answers above was a lack of parent involvement. Many of these girls experienced
the misfortune of a predator/stranger contacting
them because they failed to exercise safety precautions and their parents had not drawn appropriate
boundaries. Some were far too young to be participating on the social networking sites in the first
place! All of the situations that occurred on the
social networking sites could have been avoided had
the girls simply set their profile page to private and
required those making friend requests to know their
last name or e-mail. And in the situations involving
Instant Messenger, the parents would have been
aware had they been monitoring the conversations
through monitoring software. Note that the main
reason kids do not tell their parents when they are
contacted by a stranger online is because they fear
their parents will withdraw their Internet privileges.
Reassure your children that you will not overreact

should they come to you. The higher goal is making sure they know that they can come to you when someone makes them feel uncomfortable online. Continue to reassure them of this fact.

Many of these girls experienced the misfortune of a predator/stranger contacting them because they failed to exercise safety precautions and their parents had not drawn appropriate boundaries.

When it comes to predators, I have found that they tend to stay away from Facebook since the networks are more enclosed and most people don't associate with strangers on the site. However, I have found that the greatest danger on Facebook is the students themselves. MySpace can be a safe environment if users set their page to private and also require that those sending friend requests know their last name or e-mail. The more layers of protection, the better. Most predators won't bother contacting kids whose pages are set to private since they can find plenty of underage minors with pages open to the public. My daughter had a MySpace page (she has since deactivated it and moved on to

Facebook) for about one year from the time she was fifteen-and-a-half to sixteen-and-a-half years old. She set her page to private and was careful not ever to have a profile picture that was a close-up of her face (thumbnails of profile pictures are accessible to the public when doing a search on MySpace). I am happy to say that it paid off, and she was never contacted by a stranger the entire time she had an account on MySpace.

Too Much Information!

In a recent study by the Pew Internet and American Life Project, 79 percent of teens agreed that kids are not as careful as they should be about the information they give out online. If this doesn't raise an eyebrow among parents, I don't know what will. Why do people reveal information online that they would never share otherwise? Amanda Lenhart, senior research specialist, at the Pew Internet and American Life Project, suggests that people do so because they lack context online. "There are plenty of places in the real world where we give away personal information," she says, "but we have a context for it—we're at a friend's party and we give someone our phone number for instance. We trust that our friend would invite people to his or her party that we might have a shared interest with. It's a safe place to share information. But we lack that context online. So there is a real tension—people are saying 'I want to know you. I want the world to know me.' But because it's not physical, people think they are safe to put anything online while searching for that connection."[12]

In a recent study by the Pew Internet and American Life Project, 79 percent of teens agreed that kids are not as careful as they should be about the information they give out online.

Ms. Lenhart adds that people still believe that only the people they know will ever be interested in anything they write online.[13] Parents must be diligent in reminding their children that nothing they ever post to the Web is private. This includes social networking sites where the page is set to private, IM conversations, and the more private form of messaging available on the social networking sites. In addition, many IM conversations are saved to a file on the hard drive or tracked through monitoring software. It is also possible to take screen shots of a screen and save it to the hard drive. Even if the information is deleted, it can live on indefinitely on someone else's computer. We must drill it home to our kids that they don't have a private "space" when it comes to the World Wide Web.

As we come to a close, it is my prayer that this book has helped you in the effort to tune in to your children's logged-on lives. Most importantly, I pray that it has spurred you on to become engaged in their wired world. As is true with most things, technology can be used for good and evil. It's up to parents to train their children to discern between the two. The landscape of technology will continue to shift; and as it does, parents will continue to scramble in an effort to keep up with their tech-savvy kids. This is not a one-time pep talk. It is a full-time job.

Just recently my youngest son received a portable gaming device as a gift. I was only basically aware of its abilities and assumed it was nothing more than a souped-up Game Boy. Until, that is, my son announced within minutes of turning it on, "Cool! This gets wireless Internet! Look Mom, I just went to your MySpace page!" Oh boy. A wave of fear swept through me. Our jobs never end, do they? I *feel* your pain. We are all in this together. And on that note I must close. Tops on my to-do list is figuring out how to set the parental controls on this new gadget my son received. If only I could interest him in one of those Mattel handheld football games we used to play on the bus on the way to school. Not likely.

Don't forget to bookmark www.loggedonand tunedout.com for updated information related to the topics discussed in this book.

APPENDIX
Talking Points, Rules, and Safety Contracts

Instant Messaging

IM rules

In addition to going over the rules below with your child, I would at a minimum spot-check their activity, check their buddy list, and have them eliminate friends with inappropriate profiles. For extra credit, create an account and have your child add you to his or her buddy list so you can keep better track of what is on your child's profile. Last but not least, monitoring software is a must-have!

Suggested rules (consider having your child initial each one or post it near the computer as a reminder):

1. No IMing until homework is done.
2. Try to get in the habit of asking yourself on a regular basis: "Would what I am typing bring glory and honor to God?"
3. Limit your buddy list to people you really want to talk to from time to time. A good general rule is this: if you haven't had a face-to-face conversation with the person in the past six months, don't include him or her on your buddy list. The exception might be camp friends, relatives, or friends who have moved.
4. Consider cleaning up your buddy list at the end of each year. Delete anyone you have not IMed at some point over the past year.
5. Be careful about posting song lyrics in your profile or as your away message. If the lyrics are inappropriate, it can send a message about you to others.
6. Do people share gossip with you online? If so, don't feel special. They gossip with you because

they know you are a willing party, and that's not a compliment!

7. Misunderstandings, fights with friends that need to be worked out, etc. should always be saved for face-to-face or, at a minimum, over the phone.

8. Be careful when clicking through to links on other people's profiles. Many lead to inappropriate sites, and some can even give your computer a virus.

9. Always imagine that what you are about to type could be copied and pasted by the other person and used against you in the future. If what you are going to say is not something you are comfortable with others reading, don't type it.

10. Never log onto a friend's account or pretend to be someone you're not.

11. Never copy, paste, or forward someone else's comments to another person unless you have permission.

12. Never talk to strangers online; and to be safe, never list your last name, school, phone numbers, or any other personal information in your profile or away message.

13. If your friends use bad language, be brave and tell them to clean it up. If they keep using it, block them.

14. Make sure your screen name would bring glory to God. Stay away from using words such as hottie, pimp, sexy, and other words that are suggestive, crude, or would leave others with a poor impression of you and your character.

15. Remember that e-mail and IM messages are often misunderstood because you can't read someone's face or hear the inflection in their voice. Save your serious conversations for the phone or, better yet, face-to-face. And whatever you do, never ever ask someone out or end a relationship through IM! In fact, if you are old enough to date and in a relationship, IM should not be used when discussing more serious matters pertaining to the relationship.

16. Remember that many parents have a program installed on their home computers that can track every IM conversation, every e-mail sent or received, every keystroke typed, and every Web site visited, and then send copies of it to the parents' e-mail address. Whenever you e-mail or IM someone, there's a good chance that his or her parents will be reading it too. Most importantly, God sees it!

17. If someone you don't know tries to talk to you online, tell your parents. This also goes for

someone you do know that threatens you or says anything that makes you feel uncomfortable.

18. Don't spend all your time IMing. Every now and then, pull away and talk to friends face-to-face!

Last but not least, live by Philippians 4:8, which says, "Finally, brothers, whatever is true, whatever is noble, whatever is right, whatever is pure, whatever is lovely, whatever is admirable—if anything is excellent or praiseworthy—think about such things" (NIV).

Cell phones/text messaging

Never ever:

- talk or text while you are driving. Even if it is legal in your state, it's not worth the risk of taking your life or someone else's. At a bare minimum, get in the habit of putting an earpiece in your ear before you even start your car (if it is legal to do so).

- engage in conversation with someone you don't know. There are too many weirdos out there, and it's not worth the risk.

- post your cell phone number on your social networking page, your IM profile, your away message, someone else's wall in the context of a comment, or say it out loud for others to hear in public places.

- allow others to text people in your directory unless you know they can be trusted!
- take pictures/video clips of strangers or others without their permission.
- e-mail pictures or clips to others or upload them to the Web without permission from all parties involved.

In addition, be sure to have your child program your contact information under ICE (in case of emergency) in their phones.

Tips to Being Cell-Mannered

The following is an excerpt from my magabook *TeenVirtue Confidential* that has been adapted for this book. If your child is not into taking quizzes, adapt it into talking points.

Quiz: Are You Cell-Mannered?

The cell phone. I bet you can't imagine a day without it. Believe it or not, there are some people who would like to see you try. Cell phones make it possible to stay in touch with your friends and family every minute of every day, but a cell-mannered person knows when to say hello and when to let it go. How do you score when it comes to basic cell phone manners? Take the quiz to find out!

1. You are at a restaurant with your friends (yes, fast food still counts!), and your cell phone goes off. It's one of your friends, and you haven't seen him or her for two weeks. You . . .

a) answer the phone at the table and tell him or her to come meet you at the restaurant.

b) tell your friends, "Guys, it's Emily, and she's been at camp for two weeks. I have to get this," and you take the call but turn down your volume so as not to disturb others around you.

c) ditto to the above except you excuse yourself from the table to take the call in a quieter place so others can enjoy their meal.

2. You are in church, and you forgot to turn off your phone. It vibrates in your pocket, indicating you have a text message. You . . .

a) check it out and send a quick reply. Besides, it'll make the long sermon go by faster.

b) check to see who it is. You can call them back when the service is over and you're headed to youth group.

c) fumble in your pocket, grab it, and turn it off quickly. Next time you will leave it in the car so it never happens again. Nothing should distract you or others from giving God the time he deserves.

3. You are in a movie theater and the previews are on. Your phone vibrates, and you . . .

a) answer it and quickly, tell your friend where you are and who you're with. No one likes the previews anyway, right?

b) send a quick text to your friend telling her where you are. You can trade a few text messages before the movie starts.

c) turn your phone off. You didn't pay seven bucks to sit in a movie theater and talk or text.

4. Your plane just landed and is headed for the designated gate. You want to make sure your mom is outside waiting to meet you. You . . .

a) turn on your phone, dial her number, and begin to tell her about your trip while those around you are trapped in the cabin and forced to listen.

b) turn on your phone, dial her number, and quietly ask her if she is there. When she asks you how the trip went, you tell her that you're still on the plane and will tell her all about it when you get in the car.

c) wait until you get off the plane and dial her number when you're on your way to the baggage claim area.

5. You are talking with one of your friends, and she is sharing about her painful breakup with her boyfriend. Your phone rings. You . . .

a) tell your friend, "Hang on a sec. I have to get this."

b) check to see who it is while she's talking. You don't plan to answer it, but you need to know whom to call back when you're free.

c) ignore it. Nothing is more important than giving your friend your undivided attention.

6. You are at a party, and you were supposed to meet one of your friends, but she's not there yet. You . . .

a) dial her number while waiting in line to get some food. When she answers, you scream, "Where are you, and what is taking you so long?" You keep talking while filling up your plate and shoving nachos into your mouth.

b) dial her number and ask her when she'll be there. Everyone else in the room is busy talking, and you're feeling left out.

c) make a point to meet new people. If your friend is still not there in another fifteen minutes, you will step outside and give her a quick call to make sure everything is all right.

7. You are talking with a friend on the phone and pull into your favorite fast-food drive-thru for a burger. The drive-thru line is a mile long so you decide to go inside to order. You . . .

a) keep the conversation going while walking in, standing in line, and tell him to hold on a sec when it's your turn to order. Now that's multitasking!

b) keep the conversation going until you see that it's almost your turn to order. You tell him you will call him back after you order your burger.

c) tell him you have to go before you step into the restaurant. You don't want to interrupt others with your conversation; and besides, it's too hard to talk, pay, and eat at the same time.

8. You ride with your mom to pick your aunt up at the airport. Once in the car she and your mom begin chatting in the front seat. Your phone rings. You . . .

a) answer the phone and begin your own little chat-fest.

b) answer the phone, talk for a few minutes, and then tell your friend you need to go visit with your aunt.

c) ignore the call and join in on the conversation with your mom and aunt. You can talk to your friends anytime, but your aunt only comes to town once a year. Besides, it's rude to subject others to your conversation when they are trapped in a small space with you and unable to escape.

9. You are watching a movie with some friends, and your phone goes off. It's Mom, so you better answer. You . . .

a) answer it during the movie and talk to her while your friends are shushing you.

b) answer it and tell your mom you'll call her back after the movie.

c) step out of the room and answer the phone in a more private location. That way you can focus on what your mom is saying without interrupting your friends.

10. Your mom is asking you about your day, and your phone vibrates with a text message from your friend. She is supposed to text you the times of the movie you're planning to see that night. You . . .

a) check your phone for the text and send your friend a quick text back. Mom won't mind, right?

b) politely interrupt your mom and tell her you're expecting a text about the movie times. You ask her if it's OK if you check the message and reply.

c) ignore the message. It will still be there when you're done talking to your mom.

11. You are at a football game and talking on your phone with one of your friends during half-time. You have to go to the restroom. You . . .

a) keep on talking while taking care of business. So a few potties flush in the background—who hasn't heard that before?

b) keep talking up until it's time to walk into the stall, announcing in the restroom, "I'll call you right back. I gotta go to the bathroom!"

c) don't even think about walking through the bathroom door while still talking on the phone. I mean, it's just wrong on so many levels.

12. You are at a concert, and your favorite band is on stage. You . . .

a) dial the number of one of your friends when the band is playing her favorite song. You scream into the phone telling her where you are and hold up the phone for her to hear the song.

b) start taking multiple pictures of the band with your camera phone, thus blocking the view of others around you and distracting them from the concert.

c) enjoy the song and respect the rights of others around you to also enjoy the song. I mean, you all paid big bucks to hear the band live, so it only makes sense to fully enjoy the experience.

Count the number of As, Bs, and Cs you have.

If most of your answers are C: Congratulations, when it comes to cell phone manners, you take the prize. Not many your age fall into this category. Keep up the good work, and maybe others will learn from your positive example!

If most of your answers are B and C: You're cell phone manners could use some improvement. If you're on the phone or someone calls or texts you and you're not quite sure if it's an appropriate setting to talk, err on the side of etiquette, practice some restraint, and call or text back later when the time is right.

If most of your answers are B and A: Yikes. You err on the side of rude when it comes to cell phone manners. You're probably not being rude intentionally, and you've probably never really questioned how your behavior impacts others around you. Make a concentrated effort to think of others and kick this bad habit before it gets out of hand.

If most of your answers are A: When you look up *rude* in the dictionary, your picture is beside it. Your lack of manners and consideration of others shows that you only care about one thing—YOU! Pray and ask God to help you put others before yourself. More importantly, back it up with action. You can do it!

Social Networking Sites

Safety Contract

(Note: This assumes your child has met mini-mum age requirements.)

Consider using the tips below as an online con-tract and have your teen initial each tip as a personal pledge to honor the boundaries. Let your teen know that you will be bookmarking his or her page and checking the content from time to time. Emphasize that it is not an issue of not trusting them but rather an issue of concern for their safety.

1. Use the privacy controls and set your page to private (MySpace only). Your friends will still be able to locate you and send a request to be added to your friend list. Setting your page to private adds an extra level of protection. It sends a clear message to predators that you do not wish to be contacted by online strangers and that you desire to use the site as a means to communicate with your circle of friends. If your page is open to the public, it is the equivalent of inviting people into your bedroom and allow-ing them to rifle through your photo albums or read your journals, notes, or diaries. It becomes an open book, available to anyone on the World Wide Web, which last I checked is a network of about 938,710,929 people. (Note to parents: MySpace users

who are eighteen or older are banned from sending a friend request to users who are under sixteen unless they are able to provide an e-mail address or last name of the user. Parents should be aware that this does not safeguard against older teens, including friends of older siblings, from contacting children under sixteen.)

2. Never share your last name, city, phone numbers, screen name, e-mail address, or other information that would make it easy for strangers to identify you or contact you one-on-one (like in person!).

3. Read over your profile to see if you have disclosed information that would enable a stalker or predator to track you down. I know this sounds creepy, but try to view your page objectively through the eyes of someone who may have malicious intent. You can never assume that only "good people" are viewing your profile, even if it is set to private. They can gain access through others on your friend list or pose as someone your age (another reason to accept only your real-life friends!).

4. Make sure your pictures are appropriate. Never upload pictures in swimsuits, pajamas, or undergarments. Do not pose suggestively or seductively. It may seem funny to you, but those with malicious intent will misread it. (For more rules on

picture and video uploads, see "Pictures and Video Uploads" on page 188.)

5. Limit your friend list to real friends. Who needs five hundred or more online strangers as friends anyway? If you ask me, it's a cry for help, a flag to low self-esteem, and a sign that you have way too much time on your hands. (The exception would be band or artist-type sites who have a fan base.)

6. When it comes to the comments others post on your wall/page/pictures, remember that you will be judged by the company you keep. In other words, "you are who you hang out with." If others feel comfortable coming on your page and posting inappropriate comments, whether it's sexual banter or the f-bomb, it should be a wake-up call that a character check is in order.

7. One in five kids between the ages of ten and seventeen have been solicited for sex online. If anyone ever makes you feel uncomfortable online, tell your parents! If you receive a sexual solicitation, copy and paste it in an e-mail and send it to CyberTipline.com.

8. Keep in mind that many schools, teachers, colleges, employers, and other organizations are searching MySpace and Facebook for information about potential students or employees.

9. Remember that information you delete never really goes away. The pages are archived, and many are accessible free of charge to the public. Archive.org has a feature called "Wayback Machine" where you can enter a URL and it will list dates from the time the site was created to its current status. Clicking on a date will transport you back to what the page(s) looked like from the time the site was created. Every time you post something online, it is like leaving a trail of bread crumbs for anyone who might want to trace your journey back to its starting point, even though you are long gone!

10. When it comes to the social networking sites like Facebook and MySpace, 1 Chronicles 29:11 sums it up nicely: "Yours, LORD, is the greatness and the power and the glory and the splendor and the majesty, for everything in the heavens and on earth belongs to You. Yours, LORD, is the kingdom, and You are exalted as head over all." We would all be wise to remember that all space is really "his space." Would your page make God smile? Would others come away knowing you are a Christian?

Parents, remember that the list above is not comprehensive. If your child is young and/or lacks maturity, you might add additional safeguards such as no profile picture, no picture or video uploads allowed, no using the blog feature, no friends unless they are real-life good friends and/or you preapprove them. Again, you can limit the information they post and ban them from using many of the features offered. You can exercise control, but you must be engaged in the process in order to know how to do this.

On the following pages, I have also included some fictional scenarios that I presented in *TeenVirtue Confidential*, a magabook for teen girls. These scenarios take a futuristic look at how sharing too much information can produce devastating fallout in the years to come. I wrote them in hopes that they would serve as a deterrance when it comes to sharing too much information online. I encourage you to go over the scenarios with your daughters (and sons) before allowing them to participate in the social networking sites.

Scenario 1: You are about to graduate from law school, and your dream is to be an attorney at a large, prestigious law firm. You are invited to interview with one of the top three firms in the city where you desire to practice. The interview goes great, and they basically tell you that they have narrowed it down to two candidates, and you are one of them. Before you leave, they give strong indication that you are the front-runner. They tell you that they will call you in a few days if they are going to extend an offer. A few days go by, and the call doesn't come. Finally, you can't stand the suspense of not knowing so you pick up the phone and call the personnel director.

You politely ask her if they have come to a decision. She sounds hesitant on the phone and delivers the unfortunate news that they decided to make an offer to the other candidate. Your heart sinks. You really had your heart set on working at this firm. You were almost certain that you were going to get this job and had even told your parents that it was a done deal. Before hanging up, you work up your nerve and ask her why they decided on the other candidate. You tell the personnel director that her information could possibly help you in future interviews.

And then, she drops the bomb. "Well, if you really want to know, we had decided on you. However, we wanted to make certain that you would be a good match with the values and integrity that we deem to be important in this firm, so we decided to take a look at your Facebook page. This is a standard procedure in our firm, and we can easily access a student's page through alumni at the firm or one of our college interns. What we found on your page raised some red flags, and even though you interviewed well, we just couldn't take a chance. I'm very sorry. I only share this with you as it is very common for employers to look up potential candidates on MySpace and Facebook, and it may continue to be a factor in your not getting a job."

You are speechless, but you regain your composure, politely thank her, and hang up the phone. You pull up your Facebook page, and for the first time you view it through different eyes—the eyes of a potential employer. On your wall one of your friends has jokingly posted, "Hey Amanda, you slut! I haven't seen you in forever. Let's hang out soon!" There are plenty of other expletives and sexually suggestive comments on the page. And then there are the pictures . . . several of you drinking at a party, another one of you kissing your boyfriend, and another of you and a friend leaning over in your bikini tops exposing your cleavage for all to see. It seemed funny at the time. But you're not laughing now. Through tears you begin to remove the evidence . . . one picture and one comment at a time.

Note: The account above, while fictional, has an element of truth to it. My office (a Christian-based ministry) was recently hiring for a marketing position, and we felt it was wise to do background checks through MySpace and/or Facebook. Out of nearly twenty applicants, all but one had a profile set up on one of the sites. My office manager and

I were able to eliminate three applicants for consideration based on information found on their MySpace or Facebook pages!

Scenario 2: You meet a really nice guy who finds you on MySpace. He goes to a different high school in your city and says he's a sophomore just like you. Before long, you are talking about meeting somewhere. You're not stupid, so you set up the meeting at the mall and make sure that your friends will be there with you. The meeting time arrives, and he never shows.

When you get home later, he messages you and says that he chickened out because he didn't tell you the complete truth when you met online. He tells you that he's really older than sixteen and that he still wants to meet you if you're game. When you ask him how old he is, he tells you that he's twenty-five and that he listed the high school he used to attend and a fake age because he wants to meet younger girls.

Now you're totally creeped out, and you tell him no way will you ever meet him. He pleads with you to meet him and says that if you get to know him, he knows it will still work out. You tell him no and sign off.

The next day you head to work at the dry cleaners down the block from your school. You're excited because you are working the same shift as your best friend. The first hour is pretty busy, but then it slows down, and you and Sarah have a chance to catch up. You tell her all about the creep you met on MySpace and how you refused to meet him. She tells you to block him just to be safe, and you agree to do it when you get home. At that moment your cell phone buzzes with a text. You look, and it's a message from him. The message says, "u look hot today." Sarah is busy at the counter with a customer who just walked in. Is it him? Then you notice a guy sitting outside in a jeep, and you remember that he said he drove a jeep. He smiles at you and your phone buzzes with another text. You look down at your phone and it says, "when is ur break?" How did he know you were at work? You had told him where you worked, which you now realize was a huge mistake. You had also posted your cell phone number. And then you remembered that Sarah had posted a message to you last night saying she was excited that you guys had the same shift the next day. What else did this guy know?

You text him back and tell him to get lost—you don't ever want to meet him. You warn him that if he contacts you again, you're calling the police. He reads the text and screeches out of the parking lot. By then the customer is gone, and Sarah can tell you're upset. You tell her what happened, and she suggests that you tell your parents. You are super-scared this guy is going to stalk you, but you can't imagine telling your parents. They will ground you for life for talking to him in the first place and probably make you shut down your MySpace page. After work, on the way home, you keep checking your rearview mirror for his jeep. At one point a jeep pulls up beside you at a stoplight and you are shaking uncontrollably. You have your cell phone ready. It's not him. Finally, you pull into your drive-way. You can't live like this. You decide to tell your parents.

Scenario 3: Fast-forward ten years from now. You have met the man of your dreams, and it's time to meet his parents. You can picture yourself with this guy for the rest of your life. He is a godly man who somehow managed to stay committed to Christ though his high school and college years. You, however, have a different story. Even though you were raised going to church, you ended up in the wrong crowd in high school and partied it up. Once you got to college, you realized how empty those years were and came back to the path of God. It wasn't easy. You found a church, joined a small-group Bible study, and gave up parties and drinking. Years later your new Christian friends could hardly believe the stories you told them about your past. You deeply regret the mistakes you made in the past and are thankful for God's forgiveness.

And then you met him. He was considered the biggest catch at your church. There was hardly a girl in the college group that didn't want to go out with him. But he chose you. After a few months of dating, you told him about your past. He was understanding and reassured you that it was all behind you now. He reminded you of 2 Corinthians 5:17 that says, "Therefore if anyone is in Christ, there is a new creation; old things have passed away, and look, new things have come." This is the kind of guy girls dream of marrying. And it looks like you just might be the lucky girl.

The day before you leave, he comes over to your apartment and seems upset. He was hesitant to tell you, but finally you are able to drag it out of him. He said his mother had used a software program to pull up old cached away copies of pages on the Internet from years prior. You had heard of software like this but didn't know the extent of what it could actually do. His mom had easily pulled up your MySpace page from your high school years—even though it had been shut down long ago. She was deeply disturbed by what she saw and in need of reassurance from her son that you had really changed. He assured her that you had and that she would see for herself what a wonderful girl you are when you meet in person.

You could hardly breathe when he finished telling you. Never in a million years when you had your MySpace page did you imagine that it could come back to haunt and embarrass you years later, even after you had shut it down. You cringed as you remembered back on that period of your life. After rededicating your life, you remember how sick it felt when you pulled up your page in the months that followed. It had felt so good to get rid of it and like you were making a fresh start. But it didn't really go away.

Don't think it can happen? Think again. Stories similar to the first two scenarios are making the news almost every day. And the third scenario is highly likely, given that nothing you ever post on the Web really goes away. The capability already exists to view pages on the Web that have been changed or removed. Police detectives use it regularly when investigating crimes, and it's not unreasonable to think that the same technology will be available to the general public in the years to come.

Other questions to go over with your teens: Are you sharing too much information? Have you shared details that might enable a predator or stalker to find you, follow you, and possibly harm you? Is your page something that you would be comfortable showing to a potential employer, your pastor, neighbor, grandmother, or boyfriend's parents? Are you posting things that may come back to haunt you years later, even after you have shut down your page or removed comments and pictures? Of course, the most important question is, Would my page be pleasing to God? In fact, here is a good rule of thumb—would others who look at your page know that you are a Christian based on what they find? If you state that you are a Christian somewhere on the page, would your comments, friends' comments, links, and pictures line up with your faith. Or would they scream, "Hypocrite!" Matthew 5:16 says it best: "Let your light shine before men, that they may see your good deeds and praise your Father in heaven" (NIV).

Pictures and Video Uploads

Below you will find a set of rules that I require my children to abide by when it comes to pictures and videos they (or others) may upload to the Web.

Feel free to edit or adapt them to fit your preference. I would begin going over these rules when your child enters middle school and continue to remind them of the rules as the years progress. Even if your child is not yet allowed to participate in the social networking sites, it is not too early. They may still end up in the pictures and videos taken and posted by others. You may consider even posting the rules somewhere near your computer so they are not easily forgotten.

1. Do not upload pictures or videos of yourself or your friends in swimwear, pajamas, or anything that exposes too much skin. A rule of thumb is this: What sort of reaction would the picture/video in question get from your pastor, grandmother, or dad? Also, do not allow others to take or upload pictures or videos like the ones described above to the Web. If you find yourself in that situation, politely explain to the person who took the photo or video that it will have to be removed. (It helps if your child gets the speech down so they are able to confidently explain to their friends, "My parents will not allow me to be in pictures or videos on the Web in my swimsuit or pajamas.") Let me also note here that our sons should not be *taking* pictures of scantily clad girls at the beach, lake party, or poolside, much less uploading them to the Web. There

will be plenty of girls who are willing to smile for the camera, but this does not make it acceptable to snap their picture.

2. It is wrong to take or upload pictures or videos of people without their permission. While I realize that it is not realistic to ask your friends if you can take their picture and post it in your online album, the goal is to use good judgment. As the popularity of online photo albums and sites like YouTube increase, we will see more and more lawsuits brought by people who were either photographed or videotaped against their will or who simply did not want it posted publicly to the Web. Never take pictures or video of strangers. If you have any doubts at all about whether your friends would approve of your posting pictures or videos of them on the Web, ask them.

3. Do not engage in crude behavior. There are plenty of decent pictures and videos to be taken, so make sure you never participate in such useless and ridiculous antics as urinating in public, taking pictures or videos or having a picture or video taken while on the toilet, grabbing someone's private parts, staring down someone's pants or blouse, smashing your cleavage together, public displays of affection (making out, etc.), and other behaviors that would fall into this category. (All of

the above I mention in detail because I witnessed it firsthand in my research.)

4. If a privacy setting is provided when uploading your pictures or videos to an album (usually there is), use it so it limits the people who can view your photos and videos to your immediate friend list. But always keep in mind that adults can still view your photos, videos, and information. Many parents access their children's online profiles through their children's passwords and are able to surf freely through their friend lists.

5. Do not allow inappropriate comments to be posted by others about your pictures. If you find them, delete the comments immediately. (For example, my daughter had a picture in one of her albums and one of her friends came on and commented about how busty she looked in the shirt she was wearing. Not appropriate, especially given the fact that guys on her friend list had the ability to rifle through her photo albums. The picture had to go.)

6. Make sure your photos and videos will meet the approval of Mom, Dad, and above all, God. (Tell your children that you will be spot-checking their albums, as well as their friends' albums, from time to time, and should you find evidence that they are not abiding by the above rules, you will take away

their digital camera and ban them from posting pictures.)

In addition, you may want to go over the talking points included in chapter 5 as well as the media accounts of unfortunate picture and video uploads that garnered media attention.

For downloadable safety contracts, go to www. loggedonandtunedout.com.

Notes

Chapter 1, A Call for Parents to Log On and Tune In

1. "Media multitasking changing the amount and nature of young people's media use," Kaiser Family Foundation, 9 March 2005. Available at www.kff.org/entmedia030905nr.cfm.

2. See www.netsmartz.org/pdf/cox_teensurvey_may2006.pdf.

3. "Protecting Teens Online," *Pew Internet and American Life*, March 17, 2005.

4. Crimes Against Children Research Center's Youth Internet Safety Survey.

5. *Dateline*: December 16, 2005.

Chapter 2, Instant Messaging: The Party Never Ends

1. See www.netsmartz.org/pdf/cox_teensurvey_may2006.pdf.

2. "Teen and Online Marketing," www.webad vantage.net/tip_archive.cfm?tip_id=293&&a=1. Accessed October 10, 2003.

Chapter 3, Cell Phones: The Average Teen's Lifeline

1. See www.pewinternet.org/PPF/r/179/report_display.asp.

2. Ibid.

3. Ibid.

4. CTIA-The Wireless Association.

5. Allen Breed, "Ubiquitous message technology can be powerful tool for good and ill," *USA Today,* 16 October 2006. Available at www.usato day.com/tech/wireless/phones/2006-10-13-texting-sides.x.htm.

6. See www.pewinternet.org/PPF/r/179/report_display.asp.

7. Ibid.

8. *The Wall Street Journal.*

9. See www.wave3.com/Global/story.asp?S=5492 868&nav=0RZF.

10. See www.pewinternet.org/PPF/r/179/report_display.asp.

Chapter 4, Social Networking Sites: The Virtual Malt Shop

1. A. Lenhart & M. Madden, "Social networking web sites and teens: An overview," *The Pew Internet & American Life Project,* 7 January 2007. Available at www.pewinternet.org/PPF/r/198/report_display.asp.

2. Ibid.

3. See MySpace.com (2007). Available at www. myspace/modules/common/Pages/AboutUs.aspx.

4. See Facebook.com (2007). Available at www.face book.com/about.php.

5. "comScore releases worldwide rankings on top web properties," www.comScore.com (2007). Available at www.comscore.com/press/release. asp?id=1370.

6. Janet Kornblum, "Meet my 500 new best pals," *USA Today,* 20 September 2006. Available at www.usatoday.com/tech/news/2006-09-19friend ing_x.htm.

7. Pew source: http://newswire.ascribe.org/cgi-bin/behold.pl?ascribeid=20070104.112410&time=1 3%2000%20PST&year=2007&public=0.

8. "Meet my 5000 new best pals," www.usato day.com/tech/news/2006-09-19-friending_x.htm; accessed 20 September 2006.

9. "Ideals incubate on the Internet," www.usa today.com/news/nation/2006-10-23-students-web_ x.htm, accessed 24 October 2006.

Chapter 5, Pictures and Videos: Smile, You're on the World Wide Web!

1. "Web-based video storms the planet," www. usatoday.com/life/people/2006-12-26-yir-internet_ x.htm?POE=LIFISVA, accessed 26 December 2006.

2. For more information about safety filters, go to www.loggedonandtunedout.com.

Chapter 6, Caution—Danger Ahead! Avoiding the Pitfalls of a Digital World

1. Martha Irvine, Associated Press, "Survey tracks teens' use of social networking sites," www.indy star.com/apps/pbcs.dll/article?AID=/20070110/ LOCAL17/701100386/1012; accessed 10 January 2007.

2. "What Teens Are Doing in MySpace," excerpted from *Myspace Unraveled.* Copyright © 2006 by Larry Magid and Anne Collier. All rights reserved. Peachpit Press, www.cbsnews.com/stories/2006/09/07/print/ main1983044.shtml; accessed 7 September 2006.

3. Huffaker wrote in an academic paper, "Teen Blogs Exposed: The Private Lives of Teens Made Public," which he presented at the American Association for the Advancement of Science in February 2006.

4. Olivia Barker, "Technology leaves teens speechless," *USA Today,* www.usatoday.com/tech/news/

techinnovations/2006-05-29-teen-texting_x.htm; accessed 29 May 2006.

5. Ibid.

6. Justin Patchin and Sameer Hinduja, www.readingeagle.com/re/lifestyle/1615452.asp

7. Keturah Gray, "How Mean Can Teens Be? 'Primetime' Special Shows How the Internet Can Fuel Bullying and Fighting," http://abclocal.go.com/kgo/story?section=bizarre&id=4560512.

8. Larry Magid and Annie Collier, *Myspace Unraveled,* (Atlanta: Peachtree Press, 2006).

9. Keturah Gray, "How Mean Can Teens Be? 'Primetime' Special Shows How the Internet Can Fuel Bullying and Fighting," http://abclocal.go.com/kgo/story?section=bizarre&id=4560512.

10. Information about the safety filter and monitoring software I use can be found at www.loggedonandtunedout.com.

11. Research study by Larry Rosen at California State University, 2006.

12. Jim Ellis, Associated Press, "Too much information," www.csmonitor.com/2006/1227/p17s01-cogn.html. Commentary "Linked Up" Column from the December 27, 2006 edition; "Our scrambled sense of online anonymity" by Tom Regan, accessed 5 January 2007.

13. Ibid.